DISPLACED

ALSO BY

VALERY PANYUSHKIN

12 Who Don't Agree

Valery Panyushkin

DISPLACED

CIVILIANS IN THE RUSSIA-UKRAINE WAR

*Translated from the Russian
by Brian James Baer and Ellen Vayner*

Europa Editions
8 Blackstock Mews
London N4 2BT
www.europaeditions.co.uk

Copyright © 2022 by Valery Panyushkin
First publication 2024 by Europa Editions

Translated by Brian James Baer and Ellen Vayner
Original title: *Час волка*
Translation copyright © 2024 by Europa Editions

All rights reserved, including the right of reproduction
in whole or in part in any form.

A catalogue record for this title is available from the British Library
ISBN 978-1-78770-547-0

Panyushkin, Valery
Displaced

Cover design by Ginevra Rapisardi

Prepress by Grafica Punto Print – Rome

Printed and bound in Great Britain by Clays Ltd, Elcograf S.p.A

CONTENTS

Translator Preface - 13

Chapter 1
The Hour of the Wolf - 23

Chapter 2
Inside Four Walls - 39

Chapter 3
Escape - 55

Chapter 4
Shelter - 74

Chapter 5
Rubikus and Others - 100

Chapter 6
To the East - 115

Chapter 7
Children of War - 136

CHAPTER 8
The War and Aids - 154

CHAPTER 9
The Hippocratic Oath - 169

CHAPTER 10
A Digitized War - 191

CHAPTER 11
The New Face of Femininity - 207

CHAPTER 12
Double Enemies - 222

THE FINAL CHAPTER
We're Leaving - 241

ABOUT THE AUTHOR - 253

To my friend Mustafa Nayyem,
who suggested I write this book.
To my wife, Olga Pavlova, who brought
together the characters of this book.
To my father, Valery Panyushkin,
who will probably never read this book.

DISPLACED

Translator Preface

Valery Panyushkin, an award-winning Russian journalist, began writing this book in the first few months after Russia's invasion of Ukraine. Shocked by his country's aggression, his father's support for the war, and by the hard realization that he could no longer practice his profession in a country where all independent media outlets had been forced to close and the two words "no war" carried a prison sentence, he travelled to the southern regions of Russia, Latvia, Poland, and Germany, and began collecting the personal stories of refugees, people from all walks of life and from all over Ukraine who had been displaced by the conflict. Placed side by side in one powerful narration, these testimonies create a complex picture of the human tragedy and resilience brought on by this war and provide a glimpse of the problems to come. This book is a warning to all of us. "As it happens, anyone can become a refugee," writes the author. And adds, "*It shouldn't be this way.*" We began working on this translation in October 2022. Since then, many things have changed, but the fighting continues in what many have come to see as a war of Good versus Evil.

Translating these accounts of the refugee crisis precipitated by Russia's unprovoked invasion of Ukraine in 2022 posed a number of challenges that were at once linguistic, political and historical. Perhaps the most persistent challenge was the author's use of the present tense. Switching to the present in narratives from the past is fairly typical in Russian; it is far less so in English. The use of the present tense in this book, however, seemed intended to capture the urgency and precarity of the situations described—the events erupted without warning and the subsequent unfolding of those events seemed utterly unpredictable for the ones caught in the vortex of war. We, therefore, made every effort to preserve the book's present-tense narration, even when it strained the norms of English.

Language use is also a theme. The complex and fast-changing language politics of the region is a topic that arises repeatedly throughout the book—an inevitable consequence of a Russian-speaking journalist covering a war in Ukraine, where Russian is now the language of the aggressor, at the same time that it is the dominant language of many Ukrainians, especially from the Eastern part of the country. A central feature of Russian pro-war propaganda is that Russian-speaking Ukrainians were being discriminated against by being "forced" to use Ukrainian in various institutional settings. Efforts in many post-Soviet republics to promote the official national language, which had been in various ways marginalized during the Soviet period in favor of Russian, became a central feature of Russia's politics of resentment, weaponized by the Putin regime to foment secessionist ambitions in a number of regions. As a consequence, several individuals featured in this book react with hostility to the use of Russian or, in the case of Russian-speaking Ukrainians, make a concerted effort to use Ukrainian more in their everyday lives—for example, Alla Achasova's young son spontaneously switches to Ukrainian at home following the first wave of bombings. She follows suit.

The independence of Ukraine, which followed a national referendum in 1991, when 93% of Ukrainians voted to secede from the Soviet Union, was reflected in, among other things, the call to use Ukrainian versions of place names, rather than the Russian ones, in international publications, and in official use in other languages, e.g., Kyiv, instead of Kiev, Lviv, instead of Lvov. In some cases, it has led to the replacement of Russian imperial names with native Ukrainian ones, such as Kadiivka, in place of Stakhanov. Every chapter of the book opens with a propagandistic announcement from the Russian Ministry of Defense, in which the Russian versions of Ukrainian place names are used. We decided to preserve those spellings in these passages while using the official Ukrainian spellings in the body of the book to underscore the connection between language and politics in the region. The refusal to use Ukrainian spellings is yet another way the Russian government seeks to deny Ukraine a distinct linguistic and cultural identity and thereby its right to exist as an independent nation.

Finally, the book's journalistic focus on the current moment means, perhaps inevitably, that the complex history of the region is assumed. To provide some background, we added footnotes, where relevant. For example, when recounting the story of Anna Tsimelzon's grandmother, who was evacuated during World War II from Tallinn, Estonia, to the Ural Mountains, deep in the heartland of Russia, Panyushkin notes that she dressed up in the formal gown and high heels she had for some reason brought with her to celebrate the "liberation of her hometown." Of course, this is referring to the liberation of Tallinn from German occupation. The German occupation was, however, replaced by the re-occupation of Estonia, Latvia, and Lithuania by the Soviet army. The three Baltic States had been forcibly annexed by the Soviet Union as "constituent republics" in August of 1940, putting an end to two decades of independence. Against the backdrop of this complex history, this book traces the tangled fates of regular people, peaceful civilians who got caught in the middle of a war. This book is about the displaced.

For readers interested in the historical background, we would recommend Serhii Plokhy's *The Russo-Ukrainian War: The Return of History* (W. W. Norton & Company 2023).

My father supports the war. Amid the sea of human tragedy my country has brought down upon Ukraine and the entire world, including its own population, there is my personal tragedy: My dad, an old man of eighty-two, supports the war.

He's a good man, and I love him. He taught me how to ride a bike, paddle a canoe, and how to use a saw, a chisel, and a wood plane. He's an amazing craftsman who's spent his whole life making models for theaters and exhibition halls. He plays with my children and fixes their toys when they break—my children adore him. All his life he's been in love with my mother. And for the two years before she died of a brain tumor, he took wonderful care of her.

But now he supports the war, and we barely talk. I only ask if he's taken his medications.

When my mother died ten years ago, his grief was so profound that he locked himself in his room, coming out only to get a bite to eat or use the bathroom. He left his room no more than twice a day. And all that time he spent alone in his room he was watching TV.

Back then I worked as a journalist for the Dozhd TV network, which has since been shut down; I regularly appeared on the radio station Echo of Moscow, which has also been shut down; and I wrote for *Novaya Gazeta*, which is no longer published. I used to tell my father that he shouldn't poison his brain with all that angry nonsense aired by the official

TV networks. But my dad would tell me that he didn't really watch the news or political talk-shows—mostly soccer and programs about animals. I now think it wasn't true. Dad didn't sleep well, and the TV was almost always turned on in his room. I assume that, in addition to soccer scores and fun facts about whales and penguins, the TV was, twenty four hours a day, telling my father about spiteful Nazis who'd seized power in Ukraine, about an insatiable NATO that was encircling Russia with military bases, about transnational corporations that were buying up all of Russia's oil, about the dollar that refused to let the ruble become a world currency, and about journalist traitors (I was one of them) who slandered President Putin and his project of returning Russia to its status as an international superpower—the TV had been talking to him about all that.

A few months after Mom's death, when the pain of loss had become less acute, my father started to leave his room. He'd come to visit us, invite us over, play with the grandchildren, and talk with me. We usually chatted about everyday things, but now and then propagandistic clichés would pop up in Dad's speech: the pressure of the West, aggressive NATO, values alien to Russians, the fifth column . . .

"Dad, I'm the fifth column!"

"No, you're not! You aren't the fifth column, you're just a fool," my father would say, forgetting the fact that his son was a well-known journalist and writer, something that had once been a source of pride.

And then he'd laugh in an attempt to turn a brewing quarrel into a joke.

It seemed to me, by repeating all those propagandistic clichés, Dad was testing me to see if I'd be willing to dilute my oppositional views with a dose of commonsense conformism. I wouldn't agree, and Dad would then retreat to his previous position, that of a kindly grandpa who doesn't care about politics and spends all his time fixing broken toys for his youngest grandson.

That's how we lived until February 24, 2022, when the war began.

The first week we didn't talk about the war at all, as if we were hoping it would be over soon, like a bad dream. Then I began writing this book about refugees, and every time I'd return from my travels, I'd go to my father's and tell him about what I'd seen. I was very careful to tell him only human-interest stories, without any political commentary. I talked about people who'd lost their homes, about an old woman who'd escaped from Mariupol in the trunk of a refrigerator truck, about a boy who'd lost his brother in the war. My father would listen to the stories, sympathizing with my characters but always responding with propagandistic talking points, "Yes, but haven't the Ukrainians been fighting a war in the Donbas for the last eight years?" "Yes, but hasn't NATO surrounded Russia with their military bases?" "Yes, but hasn't the West tried to impose their own values, which are alien to the Russian mentality?" Thus spoke my father, but I kept telling my stories. I hoped to touch him with human-interest stories of misfortune that would gradually dissipate the fog of propaganda he was living in.

Then Bucha happened. I met with a refugee from this small town where more than four hundred people perished during the Russian occupation, and I wrote down her story. But as soon as I started paraphrasing this woman's account to my father, he jumped up and began screaming. He'd never screamed at me like that before, not once in my fifty-two years.

"How dare you say such things? Don't you have any decency left? How could you even think that a Russian soldier was capable of killing women and children?!"

He kept screaming, and I was afraid he'd collapse right in front of me and die of a heart attack. But suddenly I realized: He understands everything. People who don't understand what's going on or are confused by the official lies have a tendency to take an interest in what they hear, raising doubts and asking questions, especially when speaking with close friends and family. But my father was screaming in utter despair. People who react this way grasp the horrifying reality but are incapable of accepting it because that acceptance would be for them worse than death.

We are the aggressors, and that is the reality. But if we are the aggressors, what is an eighty-two-year-old man supposed to do, an eighty-two-year-old man who'd been brought up, and who'd brought his children up, on the heroic feats of those who fought in World War II, soldiers who'd gone to their death to stop aggressors? What would it mean if we were now the aggressors? It could only mean one thing—suicide.

My father was screaming, shaking, and dropping things because he understood everything, but he couldn't accept the reality. Because accepting such a reality would mean instant death or the complete destruction of his personality, and of all his values and moral beliefs.

So, I sat there without saying a word. And I thought: "Oh my God, he realizes all this is true!" Then I got up, took my coat, and walked out, leaving the old man by himself. Since then, we only talk by phone, and all our conversations are about him taking his medications.

I no longer think that my father doesn't understand what's happened. And I stopped thinking that Russians who support the war are blinded by propaganda. They are blinded, of course, but that's not the point—most of them understand everything. The point is that no one in Russia has yet to come up with a single reasonable response to the realization that we're the aggressors. There's no point suggesting public protests. In a totalitarian society, showing up at a protest is tantamount to beating your head against a brick wall; we've already tried that.

But accepting the fact that we are the aggressors is unbearably difficult. There isn't a single reasonable response that can follow such a realization, except suicide. In the first months of the war, the only thing that saved me from committing suicide was the work I'd undertaken in a state of desperation—to write this book about the refugees.

Chapter 1
The Hour of the Wolf

"As a result of strikes by Russian Armed Forces, 83 ground facilities of Ukraine's military infrastructure have been rendered inoperative. Since the beginning of the special military operation, two Su-27s, two Su-24s, one helicopter and four Bayraktar TB-2 attack drones of the Ukrainian Armed Forces have been shot down. All the tasks assigned to the Russian Armed Forces for the day were successfully completed, in particular, securing access for Russian troops to the city of Kherson." Official Representative of the Russian Ministry of Defense Igor Konashenkov, February 24, 2022.

Wars begin right before dawn. At every military school, cadets are taught that the very end of night, "the hour of the wolf," is the best time to attack, to take out the guards, to cross the border, and to bomb military targets. People are biologically wired to reach their deepest sleep right before dawn, and even those who aren't supposed to be sleeping—officers on duty, guards, border patrol—have a hard time concentrating. All cadets learn that, and when those cadets become generals, time after time they begin wars right before dawn.

Officers are not very sensitive people, and they're not concerned with historical parallels and poetic rhymes. They've probably heard Mark Bernes or Garik Sukachev singing ". . . at exactly 4:00 A.M., Kyiv was bombed, and we were told the war had begun."[1] They'd all heard this famous song but didn't realize it was no longer about Germany attacking the

---

[1] Mark Bernes (1911-1969) was a popular Soviet actor and singer most famous for his WWII songs. Garik Sukachev (b. 1959) is a popular Soviet and Russian rock musician. Both singers performed the popular song about the outbreak of World War II in the USSR, titled "On July 22, at 4:00 A.M. Sharp." It began with the lines: "Kyiv was bombed, and the war was announced . . ."

Soviet Union near 5:00 A.M. on June 22, 1945—it was about Russia attacking Ukraine near 5:00 A.M. on February 24, 2022.

The Minister of Foreign Affairs of Latvia, Edgars Rinkēvičs, wrote exactly that in a Twitter post: "Russians, this song is now about you."

The time before dawn. The hour of the wolf. Ukraine is sleeping. An explosion!

Viktoria Svetlich, a manager at Nokia, wakes up from the explosions at a hospital in Kyiv. She's in the hospital with her fifteen-year-old daughter who just underwent surgery—to implant a titanium plate in her leg. The girl can only get around on crutches. The door of her room opens, and the doctor appears. He says, "It's war. We're transferring all the seriously ill patients to the basement and discharging all those who are in recovery. Go home." But how can you go home on crutches through a city that's being bombed?

Yulia Leytes, too, wakes up in Kyiv, but in a beautiful apartment near the Opera theater. Yulia is a psychologist and a feminist. Her husband is a Russian citizen, and she worked in Moscow for a long time. She had recently returned to her hometown of Kyiv, unable to tolerate "that vague but nonetheless detectable feeling of un-freedom in the Moscow air," as she puts it. At 10:00 A.M. Yulia has a scheduled photo session for a project on the workings of violence. They're supposed to photograph broken flowers left over in flower shops. They tape them together somehow, so they resemble living flowers; they're meant to symbolize women who have survived violence. And now there's violence here, right outside her window.

Yelena Chepurnaya, a nurse, wakes up from the explosions and the howl of air defense sirens in Chernigov. She goes to the window and sees her neighbors throwing random stuff into the trunks of their cars without even putting it into bags or suitcases.

Vladimir Pavlenko, a blinds and curtains salesman, wakes

up from the explosions in Odesa. His seven-year-old daughter comes into his bedroom, "Papa, I'm afraid." What can you do—hug the girl, cuddle her on your lap? What else can you do?

Victor N., a movie producer, wakes up from the explosions on the outskirts of Kyiv and opens Facebook, where his whole newsfeed is peppered with the words "war, missiles, bombing." Victor can't see the bombing; he can only hear the rumble from afar.

Alyona Klyuchka, a clerk at the city hall of Tsyrkuny, a small town near Kharkiv, wakes up from the explosions and says to her husband:

"Andrey, it's war!"

"It can't be, go back to sleep," her husband answers, then turns on his other side and falls asleep.

Oksana K., a housewife in the same town of Tsyrkuny, wakes up from the explosions but thinks that someone has set off some incredible fireworks. So, she gets dressed to go outside to watch them.

"Where are you going?" asks Oksana's husband, the owner of a small shop that makes massage tables. He stops her: "Stay inside! The war's started! Get the children ready."

Oksana runs around the house, packs their bags, wakes up their children—two boys, one three and the other five—gives them something to eat, gets them dressed, then dresses herself. And here they are—standing with their children in their arms and their packed suitcases in tow not knowing where to go. They have a car, but there's only enough gas to go a hundred kilometers, and no one knows where to go. Is it possible to go west? What if you end up in the middle of the battle for the Kharkiv ring road? The town of Tsyrkuny is only a couple of kilometers from Kharkiv, and you can hear the sounds of the fighting. Oksana peeks outside and sees Russian tanks on the streets. There's only one option left: go back home and wait for who knows what.

In the same town of Tsyrkuny, Lyubov Alexandrovna and Nikolay Petrovich, elderly retirees, are awakened by the explosions and the sound of breaking glass. Yesterday their grandson arrived with his wife and fourteen-year-old daughter, their great-granddaughter. Today is her birthday, and they were planning to celebrate it with her great-grandmother and great-grandfather. The roar and the ringing that woke them up was from a shell that fell right into their vegetable garden, shattering their two large glass greenhouses. Their backyard is now covered with broken glass, and when the sun rises, it will sparkle like an ad for Swarovski crystal.

Only Alla Achasova sleeps. She's a soil scientist living in Kharkiv. Despite the roar of the explosions outside, she's asleep, and dreaming. When she tells me about that dream, she feels embarrassed—it's all so silly, but for some reason the refugees love talking about their dreams, and many believe they're prophetic. In her dream, Alla is swimming on a small ice floe on a cold and gloomy sea. The ice floe is about to melt and fall apart, which means death. Alla is unable to steer the ice floe, and the current and the wind drive the ice floe toward an island surrounded by sheer rocks. Alla can't climb onto the rocks. The ice floe is drifting among the rocks, but they're inaccessible—there's no hope. It's an anxious, uneasy dream, but suddenly Alla sees embedded in the rocks a castle or a cathedral—she's not sure what to call it. It has black walls with the streak of yellow, there's a tower, and a wide gate framed by heavy columns. In her dream, Alla steps from the ice floe through the gate and walks along a road paved with light stones. Once inside, she sees a garden, tables laden with food, and welcoming people—in a word, salvation. At this point Alla wakes up, and the reality is more terrifying than her nightmare.

Vacation Requests

What do people do when they wake up under bombardment? It's hard to believe, but they go to work. Many businesses are organized in such a way that it's impossible to halt operations. You can't stop a blast furnace, for example. Even when a war breaks out, air-controllers can't leave their workstations until the last civilian plane has left the airspace under their control. And then there are the doctors... A fifteen-year-old girl is lying in Kyiv's Center for Maternal and Infant Care (Okhmatdet). Her name is Katya; she's been diagnosed with acute lymphoblastic leukemia, blood cancer, and is being prepared for a bone marrow transplant. Over the past week, Katya's bone marrow has been intentionally destroyed by toxic drugs so that it can be replaced with stem cells from Katya's sister. If they cancel the surgery now, Katya will die. That's why, despite the shelling, the doctors go to work and finish the scheduled surgery. The fact that they continue working is only to be expected.

But other people go to work too—those who are not responsible for either human lives or life-supporting infrastructure, or even for equipment in need of constant attention. In Odesa, the curtain salesman Vladimir Pavlenko loads his car with inventory samples and drives to meet a client at 11 in the morning, as they agreed the day before. There are already antitank hedgehogs in the center of the city, on Deribasovskaya Street. The militia draft offices are already signing up volunteers and distributing weapons to civilians. With the naked eye you can see Russian military ships in the harbor. Russian military planes are flying overhead. But Vladimir arrives at his client's house and arranges his "anti-sun systems" on the table in front of her.

"Do you really think now is a good time to pick out blinds? Our windows could be shattered at any moment."

"I don't know," Vladimir answers. "But we agreed yesterday."

This is how he answers, and for some time they look through his curtain samples and discuss the best way to dress windows in a city where it's better to stay as far away from windows as possible.

People just won't believe their lives are destroyed. They continue to go about their everyday routine automatically, the same way a drowning person tries to inhale under water.

For some time, Yulia Leytes insists that the photo shoot of broken flowers can't be canceled, and only when the photographers, lighting engineers, and studio owner refuse to continue does she put her headphones on. They are very good noise canceling headphones. She puts them on, selects her favorite music, and goes to say goodbye to her father and grandmother. She walks through the center of Kyiv and hears nothing, as if there is no war.

The movie producer Victor N. leaves his wife and nine-year-old daughter at home and drives to his office to pick up papers and finish some work. After that, he drives to his business partner's home located not far from the Gostomel airport, in the Bucha region, to settle some additional matters. And that's where he spends the whole day until evening. Victor is still at his partner's place at the start of the curfew, so he calls his wife to tell her that he's not coming home until tomorrow. And he can't really grasp the fact that he left his wife and daughter alone in a city under attack, and that right now, only two kilometers from where he's staying, there's a battle taking place—one of the fiercest battles of the start of the war, the battle for Bucha.

In Chernigov, the nurse Yelena Chepurnaya, too, goes to her job. She works at a regular outpatient clinic, so she doesn't have patients in the middle of a bone marrow transplant. Today, Yelena doesn't have any patients at all. Only two old people from the suburbs—they must've left home very early, before dawn, and so knew nothing about the war. It's impossible to help them because all the hospitals have stopped accepting even scheduled patients. The outpatient clinic is empty; all personnel have been sent home. The only one left is the head of HR, who's in a state of extreme agitation. He's running through the hallways and trying to find the paperwork that has to be completed before all the doctors, nurses, nurse's aides, and coat room attendants exit the clinic.

"Please, submit a vacation request," he keeps saying. "Please, before you leave, everybody needs to fill out a vacation request."

Yelena turns in her vacation request and goes home. She tries to call her mother and brother, who live in the countryside. They don't answer their phones. She tries calling her daughter in Kyiv. The daughter says she's fine and tells Yelena to leave immediately for western Ukraine. Not far from Yelena's home, the airfield has been destroyed by bombs and is now on fire. But the bridge through the Desna River is still intact. Two weeks later, it will be riddled by Russian artillery, and then, to prevent the advance of the Russian army, Ukrainian artillery will completely destroy it. The only road west will be gone. In Chernigov, half of the buildings will be destroyed by bombing and shelling. Some missiles will hit the outpatient clinic where Yelena used to work. The fate of the vacation requests dutifully submitted by the staff remains unknown. Were they incinerated? Were they scattered by an explosion? Or were they securely stored away in the basement by the head of HR? Whatever the case may be, they're now overdue, and who knows why it was so important to fill them out, wasting precious time.

People just can't believe their lives are destroyed, so they continue to follow their everyday routines.

In Kharkiv, the soil doctor Alla Achasova wakes up after her dream about the ice floe and talks on the phone with her children's teacher about them missing school today. Then she makes breakfast for her husband and children. Then she puts on her work clothes (but keeps her slippers on) and takes part in a Zoom-conference on soil erosion. Alla is a member of an international group of scientists established by the UN to study global warming. On February 24, 2022, these scientists are discussing in English the connection between global warming and soil erosion. Alla listens to them from Kharkiv, where in the very near future only missiles will plow the soil, and the main cause of soil erosion will be the movement of tank columns. Alla listens and makes an occasional comment. Until her neighbor begins knocking on her door:

"Alla, what are you doing? There's a battle on the ring road! Get up, we've got to go to the basement."

They run. The Kharkiv ring road, for which a fierce battle will be waged over the course of many days, can be seen from Alla's multi-storey apartment building.

That Bitter Language

From the first hours of the war, Alla receives texts from the local authorities on her phone—"Air raid alarm, go to a bomb shelter," "Don't go outside, there are clearing operations in the city"—as well as a map with the location of bomb shelters. The basement in Alla's building is on that map, as is the basement of the building next door. But both basements are filled with water. They're not just damp, no, the water is up to your knees. The metro stations, too, are marked as bomb shelters, but the one nearest to Alla's house is the last station on the Alekseyevskaya line. This station is new and not very deep, plus you have to walk for fifteen minutes under shelling to get there. Alla decides to stay home and put her children in the entryway, far away from the windows. She tells her nine-year-old son: "Go to the entryway and sit on the floor! Hurry!" Her other son, the fifteen-year-old, isn't home, and neither is her husband. The only other person there is her imperturbable mother-in-law, who wanders from one room to another. She's very old and can't hear a thing. For her the war hasn't begun yet. She asks, "Alla, why didn't the children go to school?" At this very moment the rumble outside becomes so loud that even she can hear it. "Oh Lord," says the old woman. "Is it war?" She mumbles something in a low voice, probably a prayer, and goes to sit next to her grandson in the entryway. Alla's older son and husband are still not home.

The shelling lasts for ten minutes, then twenty; the walls are shaking. Alla checks her social media. In the neighborhood chatroom someone writes that his windows have been blown out, another writes that metal shards that look like pieces of rebar flew into his apartment and pierced the walls. And someone else writes that there's a dead body lying on the ground in the courtyard—please, come and identify it if you're missing a relative. And her husband and older son are still not there, and they don't answer their phones. In an attempt to calm her nerves, Alla takes some valerian root tincture, but it doesn't help. Then she chases the valerian root with some cognac.

Finally, the front door opens, and there on the doorstep are her older son and husband. Each of them is carrying several five-liter containers of drinking water. They risked their lives to get that water, even though the plumbing is still working. As is the heating, electricity, cellphones, and internet—for now. The younger son sits on the floor and doesn't pay any attention to the explosions—he's too busy playing Minecraft on his phone; or maybe it's some other game. The war outside seems no more real to him than the war on his phone. After all, his mom gets her information about the war mostly from social media. "Mom, why are you so worried?" asks her younger son. Her older son and husband are very proud of themselves—they brought drinking water sealed in containers. This seems very important even though no one can yet imagine that in the basements of Mariupol people will be completely without water or will have to drink water from the sewer.

Alla doesn't have any food reserves. She refused to succumb to the pre-war panic and so didn't buy anything extra. All she has now is an opened bag of buckwheat, some millet, rice, pasta, flour, and a few canned goods—enough for two or three days, maybe a week. On the second or third day of hiding in the entryway, Alla will risk going outside. Taking advantage of a lull in the shelling, she'll make her way to the nearest food store. There she'll buy the only product left on the barren shelves—raisins. On the third or fourth day, somehow a bread delivery will be organized, and humanitarian aid will arrive. Alla's husband will get up before dawn to wait in line for bread, ignoring the cold and the air raid sirens. The shelling will not disperse the bread lines.

Using the excuse that he's helping his father get food for the family, Alla's older son will sneak outside and wander the streets, trying to observe the war with his own eyes. One of those times, a missile will fall dangerously close to him. This will put a stop to his excursions once and for all. On that same day, he will switch to Ukrainian when talking to his mother, even though the Anchasovs are a Russian-speaking family. For Alla, too, her mother tongue will acquire a bitter taste, and she'll begin speaking Ukrainian to her children.

Ethnically, Alla is Russian. She was born in Crimea. One of her favorite groups on social media is made up of her Crimean classmates; it lets them stay in touch and share happy memories from their childhood. On the first day of the war, her Crimean classmates began writing to Alla, telling her that she wasn't seeing the whole picture: "Russia didn't attack you, Russia is defending itself—it's you who've been bombing the Donbas for eight years." Or: "The Russian armies aren't occupying you; the Russian armies came to free you. You just don't understand." And Alla is reading all of this while sitting on the floor in her entryway, leaning against a wall shaking from the explosions.

Another important online group for Alla is one for adoptive parents. Alla's older son was adopted. People who adopted orphans from Russia, Ukraine, and Belarus try to stay in touch and help one other; they share their experiences and organize teaching seminars or just celebrations. On the day the war began, this chat group of like-minded people broke into three parts. The Russian adoptive parents (not all of them, of course, but some) began fiercely to argue that Russia wasn't attacking but defending Ukraine, that Ukraine was waiting for her Russian rescuers, that for the last eight years the Ukrainians had been bombing the Donbas. "Who was bombing the Donbas? Me?" Alla tries to reason with them. "Don't you remember how we evacuated the orphans from the Donbas—you took them East, and I took them West." But no, they couldn't hear her.

The adoptive parents from Belarus cautiously show their support and suggest that Alla and her family evacuate to their homes in Minsk. From Kharkiv, it's closer than Poland. But their offers are hardly reassuring. How can you invite Ukrainian refugees to Belarus when Russian armies entered Ukraine from there?

The Ukrainian adoptive parents are more insistent with their invitations. *Come to our place, come to our place! Come to Ivano-Frankivsk! Come to Chernovtsy!* "Come to our place in Dnipro city!" says her good friend Maya Baranova, the headmaster of the Dnipro orphanage.

Their food is almost gone, but the shelling hasn't stopped. They've spent ten days on the floor in the entryway. To calm his nerves, Alla's husband practices some breathing exercises; they help him to sleep at night. Alla hasn't slept for ten days. And finally, she makes up her mind—she will leave with the children for Dnipro.

A Train in the Dark

Alla doesn't have a car. They say there are some evacuation trains leaving from the railway station. But Alla doesn't know when and where. Actually, there's the Ukrainian Railways site uz-vezevo.com, which provides lists of passenger transportation during the war. Every night the site posts the train schedule for the following day. On the day Alla plans to leave the city, there are eleven trains departing from the railway station—to Lviv, to Ivano-Frankivsk, to Dnipro, to Khmelnitsky, to Uzhgorod. Some trains are free, others require tickets. But Alla can't find the site. For some reason it doesn't show up when she does a Google search under "evacuation trains from Kharkiv," and no other searches bring it up. Neighbors suggest that she just go to the railway station and wait there for a train.

The railway station is fifteen kilometers from Alla's house. Public transportation isn't working. And you can't walk there under shelling. The neighborhood chat provides a list of "thirty heroic cabdrivers" (that's exactly how they're referred to). Those cabdrivers will take people around the city, but for an astronomical price. Nonetheless, Alla calls them, but the heroic drivers don't answer or refuse to pick her up as she lives very close to the ring road, where the battle is now raging.

Then Alla begins calling her acquaintances to see if someone is going to Dnipro by car and can take them along. After about fifty calls, she finds some friends who are going and, yes, they have room for three more people, and yes, they'll take them tomorrow. When Alla calls the next day, the friends say they've postponed the trip until tomorrow. Then for another day. And then another. When Alla calls the fourth time, the friends say, "Sorry, we already left—we're in Kremenchug now."

Finally, someone from the neighborhood chat gives Alla the number of a priest, Andrey Pinchuk—he transports refugees on a small bus, and his driver is someone named Yan, a psychologist and a hospital clown who used to entertain children with cancer before the war.

Alla calls him. The priest's voice is tired but calm. The next morning, he and the hospital clown pick up Alla and her children. The only drawback—you can't take any luggage with you, only one medium duffle bag. For another hour the small bus will drive around the city, picking up more refugees. The bus is filled to the roof with people—if everyone had brought a large suitcase, all of them would not have fit. As they leave the city, a few more buses join them, and they drive in this small column to Dnipro. And there in the city of Dnipro . . .

"Hey, mom! Look, the trams are working!" exclaims Alla's younger son.

In Dnipro, the stores are open and even pharmacies are working. You can hear the air raid sirens—and everyone obediently goes to the bomb shelters—but there is no bombing. A persistent and hopeful rumor circulates that because the Golden Rose Synagogue, the biggest synagogue in Europe, is located in Dnipro, on Sholom Aleichem Street, and because the billionaire Roman Abramovich is taking part in the negotiations between the Ukrainians and the Russians primarily to save that synagogue, Dnipro is not being bómbed. Everyone wants to believe this.

Nevertheless, the orphanages in Dnipro are being evacuated. There is a whole train reserved for orphans, for large families (with three or more children under 18), and for families with adopted children. But Maya Baranova, an orphanage director and Alla's friend who took in Alla and her sons, can't evacuate—her husband is seriously ill and almost incapable of walking on his own. Maya can't leave her husband, and so she gives Alla and her sons her place on the children's train.

The train moves in complete darkness. The engine lights are turned off, and there are no lights in the windows. They travel in sleeping cars, three people per berth. Conductors bring tea and packages of instant mashed potatoes, which are ready to eat after adding hot water. When a kid turns on his cellphone to check TikTok or play some game, the conductor runs through the car, yelling and screaming, "What are you doing? Turn it off! Turn it off! They'll bomb the whole train!"

The Church of Saint Martin

They spend a night in Lviv. A gym was hurriedly converted into a temporary shelter for refugees. There are mattresses on the floor. There are either no sheets on the mattresses or so many people have slept on the same sheets that Alla is worried they might get scabies or lice. Alla's younger son gets ready to sleep on one of these questionable mattresses and asks:

"Mom, does Putin have any children?"

"Yes, Putin has children," Alla answers. "But he doesn't have a soul."

The next morning buses take the passengers from the children's train to the Polish border. There's a long line, but their documents are quickly checked and there they are—in Poland. As soon as Alla steps onto Polish soil, she feels enveloped by a wave of maybe not happiness but of warmhearted welcome. Volunteers . . . There are volunteers everywhere offering them coffee, food, clothes, blankets, and toys for the children. They invite them into a warm tent and tell them about the places they can go by bus from the camp.

Soon all the passengers from the children's train arrive at the refugee shelter in the small town of Kostelec nad Orlicí. Alla settles in, makes sure her children are comfortable, and then goes to the communal kitchen to make some food. There is a woman in Muslim garb near the stove. Alla says hi, and the woman greets her in return. They don't really talk, just some polite conversation—Who are you? Where are you from? Then, suddenly, without raising her voice, in a calm and somewhat detached manner, this woman in Muslim clothing begins to tell her story. She, too, is a refugee, but she's been a refugee since 1994, when the First Chechen War began. Since then, she's been wandering through shelters and refugee camps. She lost two sons. And this is what she says: "Well . . . the armies aren't so bad," this Chechen woman explains. "The armies attack each other. Be afraid of the mercenaries—the mercenaries attack civilians."

Before Alla could get her head around the idea of spending twenty-eight years as a wandering refugee and losing two children, she receives a text from her husband. It turns out, many European universities have announced they are hiring scientists from Ukraine. And it turns out, many universities have a need for soil experts. Her husband's text contained an attachment with a long list of professors who are ready to collaborate. Alla recognizes some of the names—she knows them through their publications. She wants to work at the Research Institute of Soil and Water Conservation in Prague most of all. One phone call and Alla learns they're ready to accept her there. Jan Mašek, a researcher at that Institute, is, unfortunately, sick with COVID, but his wife is ready to welcome Alla and her children. They can stay in Jan's mother's apartment, to start, and Alla can begin working as soon as April 1.

"When can you be in Prague?" Jan asks, in between coughs.

But what refugee can know for sure where and when? After two and a half weeks of war, Alla has lost the ability to plan ahead for more than two hours. When will I be in Prague? I'll go now and ask if there are busses from Kostelec to Prague. If there are, I'll get on the first bus with available seats. Or I'll get there some roundabout way. How long can such a detour take? Oh, those detours can take a very long time. Alla and Jan keep talking, and it becomes obvious that, for all his compassion, the Czech scientist can't yet grasp just how precarious the world has become for this refugee from Kharkiv.

One way or another, Alla finds a bus to Prague and makes it to the Czech capital with her children. Jan's wife meets them and takes them to Jan's mother's apartment. The next day Alla goes looking for a refugee center to register, get an assistance package, and sign the children up for school, at least temporarily.

It's already spring in Prague. The trams are cheerfully clicking along the streets, customers are walking out of stores, lovers are strolling hand in hand, and old people are sitting on benches—why don't people appreciate such happiness!

Alla walks through this city where she's never been before, steps onto an unknown street, and suddenly—she sees it. There it is! There's no mistaking it! Alla remembers it exactly. In the middle of the street, right in front of Alla, stands the Savior Castle from her dreams—black walls tinged with yellow, a tower, and wide gates framed by heavy columns. Next to the castle is a plaque for tourists explaining that the Savior Castle from her dreams is called the Church of St. Martin in the Wall.

For the sake of accuracy, it should be pointed out that the refugee center in not exactly inside that castle, but nearby.

Chapter 2
Inside Four Walls

> "Russian servicemen delivered more than 40 tons of humanitarian aid to residents of the Kiev Region. Food and other essential products were delivered to settlements controlled by the Russian army. The aid included grains, canned meat and fish, confectionary and baked goods, candies and sweets, and bottled water. The entire humanitarian cargo was distributed to residents of settlements in the Kiev Region." Official Telegram Channel of the Russian Ministry of Defense, March 13, 2022.

DOING SILLY THINGS

Civilians can't prepare themselves for life during war—it's a totally absurd idea. Civilians shouldn't be in wars. After the first shots were fired, this was drilled into civilians' heads by all kinds of experts. The government sent texts—*Run away! The war bloggers screamed on Facebook and YouTube—Run away, run away! If you're not in the army or militia, if you're not a Red Cross volunteer—run away! You aren't only putting your life and the lives of your family members in danger, but you're also getting in everybody's way. The soldiers are afraid to shoot because they know there are still a lot of civilians around. The militias will have to rescue you instead of helping the army. The Red Cross volunteers will have to bring you humanitarian aid instead of bringing medical supplies for the wounded. So, run away, you silly people!* But few people run away in the first days of a war. Only the invading army can organize an orderly and timely evacuation of civilians, not the defending army. The people you see in the kilometer-long traffic jams on the outskirts of cities represent only a tiny percentage of the people who should run away. Most people stay and try to prepare for life in wartime.

And this is totally absurd. Life in wartime will eventually take a form, but not the way they show it in the movies, or the way your grandma recounted it. In Bucha, Gostomel, and Mariupol, people buy sugar and buckwheat, but no one buys camping pots and portable heaters—it doesn't cross anyone's mind that there won't be any heat and they'll have to cook on an open fire. Civilians always make silly mistakes when they try to organize things for life in wartime.

Yulia Leytes strolls through her native Kyiv in her trendy headphones that cancel all outside noise, filling her ears with beautiful music as if there was no war at all. She doesn't hear the explosions—instead she hears melodies. Khreschhatyc Street is not yet cut off by cement blocks and antitank hedgehogs. Well, yes, on Bolshaya Zhitomirskaya Street—which Yulia decided to walk down—people are hurrying to load their cars with suitcases, but those are Louis Vuitton suitcases and the cars are all new and expensive, with paint that is not yet scratched by missile shards and with windows that are not yet shattered. Yulia loiters. Her mom calls:

"Where are you? Go home right now! And stay home. This is a blitzkrieg—Putin will win in a couple of days. Just stay home for a while! Just stay home!"

Oh, yeah, there's a war, Yulia recalls. *I should buy some food, stock up.* And so, she goes to a fashionable bakery and buys eight croissants. Damn it, eight croissants—with chocolate, almonds, and apricot fillings—to wait out the war!

Marina Polishchuk, who works for an advertising agency in Kyiv, seems to behave more rationally than Yulia Leytes. In the early morning of February 24, Marina and her fiancé go to the nearest supermarket and fill two big shopping carts with food staples: buckwheat, rice, sugar, and canned goods. The supermarket is extremely crowded. The checkout line takes about forty minutes. Marina's children from her first marriage, girls of six and eleven, didn't get enough sleep, so they're tired, scared, and acting up. What can they do with them? They can't leave them home alone, can they? People are irritated and snap at one another, arguing about who should take the last bag of flour or about their place in the checkout line. But Marina is resolute: she remains in line and brings home at least a month's supply of food. Then, as she makes her way back home, she stops by the small food store on her block and asks the owner to post updates in the neighborhood chatroom about food deliveries.

When Marina finally reaches the multi-storey apartment building they call home, her younger daughter breaks into hysterics:

"Mama, we can't use the elevator! They told us not to use the elevator when there's fire or a war."

It's true, Marina, too, has been receiving texts from the local authorities warning against using elevators during shelling. The children were told the same thing in the safety classes held regularly at their school and kindergarten.

"Mama, we can't use the elevator!"

Marina's fiancé has gone to work to remove money and documents from the safe. And now Marina has to drag this month's supply of food to their apartment on the sixteenth floor on her own. Perhaps it would've made more sense to buy less food?

After dragging the food to the sixteenth floor, Marina makes dinner for herself and her children. Marina puts food on their plates, sits down at the table, and suddenly realizes that she can't eat a thing. She literally can't force any food down her throat—it's her body's reaction to stress. The children too don't eat anything—that's how scared and stressed out they are. So, to keep herself and the children busy, Marina begins cleaning the apartment, top-to-bottom. She dusts all the books she never had time to read, then cleans all the dishes in the cupboard that were pretty clean to begin with.

Marina leaves Kyiv on the second day of the war, abandoning almost all her food supplies. So, did it make sense to buy them in the first place and waste what precious time the refugees had left?

Karina Kovalchuk is a housewife, slim and petite. She lives with her five-year-old son in the Obolonsky district of Kyiv. Karina's husband is a singer, and he's currently on tour in Romania. Without her husband, Karina feels completely lost. Plus, she can't sleep—as soon as she falls asleep, she has nightmares about pitiless soldiers breaking into her apartment, and she instantly wakes up.

Her husband calls from Romania every hour. On the second day of the war, he calls and says that his friends have settled in the basement of a nearby building. They have enough food for several days, so one of them will come and take Karina and their son there. Karina packs a huge suitcase, which she can't carry by herself and the contents of which, most of them at least, she'll never use. Her husband's friend comes over, picks up the boy in one arm and drags the suitcase with the other. When they step outside, they hear air raid sirens. And at this moment Karina asks their rescuer if there's enough vegetarian food in the basement. Karina is a vegetarian, and so is her husband. What if her husband's friends are going to cook buckwheat with canned meat? No, they need to stop by a store now, despite the howling sirens, wait in line, and buy the last three vegetarian products left in the store—sweet rolls, cucumbers, and tomatoes.

Tatyana B., who lives in Kharkiv, is a housewife and the mother of three children; her husband is a driver. Sitting with her children in the entryway, she's afraid to go outside to get bread. So, she decides to bake some herself. They have no electricity, the internet is spotty, but there is gas, flour, yeast, and water—what else do you need to make bread?

Tatyana mixes the dough, waits for it to rise, then puts the loaf in the oven. But, for the first time in her life, the bread doesn't come out right. It spreads, breaking down into stony lumps and disgusting mucus-like slush. Tatyana starts a new batch, but the result is the same. Everyone has always praised Tatyana's baking. This is some kind of curse. Of course, on all the culinary blogs, bakers and pastry chefs say that you can make good bread only when you're in a good mood and have an open heart. But has anyone ever considered that advice anything more than idle chatter? Apparently, it's true—an unhappy person is incapable of making bread. In the hands of an unhappy person, the dough spreads and breaks down into lumps and slush. It's not worth the effort.

Run away, people! Don't waste the precious time you have left on those unavoidable silly things every civilian does at the beginning of a war. Isn't that right?

No, it's not right. Here is Anna Tsimelzon, a chemistry teacher from London and a volunteer for the international group Rubikus, which helps refugees find ways to escape—trains, buses, settlement locations, housing, and anything else that might be useful. Well, Anna Tsimelzon believes that the silly things civilians do in the first days of a war are sacred.

Anna's grandmother fled from the Nazis, traveling from Tallinn to the Ural Mountains. What could a social butterfly from Estonia, which had been under Soviet occupation for just one year, know about the Urals? Most likely, she wouldn't be able to point them out on a map. Moreover, the evacuation train didn't take her to a major city like Sverdlovsk but to a tiny town with a name the girl had never heard before. And she, too, made a mistake typical of all civilians at the beginning of a war—she packed an evening dress, fishnet stockings, and a pair of high-heel pumps. What do you need all that for in the wartime Urals? But no matter how hungry she was or how hard and dirty the jobs she had to take on just to feed herself, the young woman didn't sell her evening gown, and she guarded the pumps and stockings as her most precious possessions. She put on this outfit just once—on September 2, 1944—the day the Soviet army took Tallinn. The girl put on her evening dress and went with her girlfriend to a restaurant in Sverdlovsk. With the last of their money, they celebrated the liberation of their hometown from the Nazis.[2] And at that restaurant, Anna Tsimelson's grandmother met Anna's grandfather—her destiny, the love of her life. So, the dress turned out to be very useful.

We don't know what future role has been assigned to Yulia Leytes's croissants, to the food left behind by Marina Polishchuk, to the vegetarian rations of Karina Kovalchuk, or to the soggy bread of Tatyana B. I see the silly things civilians do in the first days of war as a kind of prayer—a prayer for a world where there's plenty of clean water, where people bake bread, and where children are well-fed, a world where you eat croissants with almonds and apricot jam and wear evening gowns with fishnet stockings and high-heel pumps. Look at these people, Lord! These silly things are prayers directed to you.

Resignation and Despair

Even though the texts sent out by the local authorities strongly recommended that civilians hide in bomb shelters, most people spent only the first days in their basements and only in those cities that were occupied or under heavy shelling, like Mariupol, or that were being purged and pillaged, like Bucha.

For a while, people try to equip their basements. In the village of Tsirkuny near Kharkiv, two kilometers from the radial road, where intense fighting is taking place, Alyona Klyuchka gets a call from a family member who lives across the street:

---

[2] After the "liberation" of the Baltic States of Estonia, Latvia and Lithuania from the German army, they were reoccupied by the Soviet army. The three Baltic States had been forcibly annexed by the Soviet Union as "constituent republics" in August of 1940, putting an end to two decades of independence.

"You don't have a cellar. Come over here."

With her husband and thirteen-year-old son, Alyona runs across the street, which is already patrolled by Russians. Soon the term "run across" will assume an ominous meaning. The neighborhood chat rooms will be full of messages like "he ran across and they shot him." But the war's just begun, the soldiers are still inclined to spare civilians, and so Alyona and her husband and son successfully make it across the street.

Their relatives' cellar is big, as cellars go, but not big enough to house five people. And it's cold—the temperature is just above freezing—and it's damp. On the shelves are jars with pickled cucumbers and tomatoes from last fall. Potatoes and beets from last year's harvest are there in boxes. Alyona's husband and their host are trying to take all this out of the cellar, so they'll have more room. The host brings wooden boards to cover the damp cement floor. They bring a small iron stove, make an improvised flue and connect it to a ventilation shaft. Then they bring some chairs—it's better than sitting on the floor; they arrange mattresses on the wooden boards—it's better than sleeping directly on the wood. The mattresses quickly get damp, but overall the place looks cozy. You can sit on the chairs, look at the fire, and try to connect to the internet to find out from news or social media if the Russians have already captured Kharkiv. Everyone is very quiet, looking at their cellphones. All the refugees say the same things: In the first days of the war, the people in the basements were mostly quiet; they barely spoke to one another, except for some short housekeeping interactions: "Add more wood in the fire." "We need to bring more water." "Give this blanket to the boy." "They say the TV tower is destroyed." And then there's quiet.

At the same time in all Ukrainian cities—at least, in the north, east, and south—people try to make non-residential buildings livable. In Kharkiv, they set up tents inside the metro stations. In Chernigov, they build wooden rails so an old man in a wheelchair can enter. In a Mariupol basement they boil water because one woman is in labor and a baby will be born any minute.

In Kyiv, Marina Polishchuk decides not to move permanently into the underground parking garage in their building and to go to the basement only when they announce an air raid. But the air raid alerts come several times a day, and as we remember, Marina lives on the sixteenth floor, and her daughters refuse to use the elevators. Three to four times a day Marina and her children go from the sixteenth floor to the basement carrying bags with necessities, and then they return to their apartment, climbing the stairs from the basement to the sixteenth floor. Finally, when they hear the sixth or seventh alarm, Marina decides to stay in the apartment and wait out the alarm in their entryway. Exhausted by walking up and down the stairs, her girls agree, even though in school they've been taught in their safety classes to go to the basement during shelling. This is a kind of resignation. The time comes when a person says: *That's it, I can't go on.*

A person can say "I can't go on" not only with words but also with their whole body. In words, Karina Kovalchuk tells her husband when he calls from Romania that, yes, it's better for her and their five-year-old son to stay deep under ground and to come outside only to take a phone call. But in reality, Karina is getting sick. She has a high fever, joint pain, and a cough, and there's no medicine. Her boy feels sick too. Now Karina can tell her husband that she's leaving the basement because they have medicine in the apartment. But, in reality, it's Karina's and her son's bodies, not their minds, that are talking through the fever and chills: "I can't go on. What happens, happens."

Karina takes her monstrous suitcase and drags it back home. This time their friends refuse to help her do something they see as unreasonable. The streets are empty. Karina can't manage to drag her suitcase across the tram rails. She tries again, and again, but in vain. Finally, a man appears walking along the tram tracks; he's wearing a hooded jacket, so she can't see his face. Karina is scared: *What if he's a looter?* But she asks him for help anyway: "Please, help me carry this suitcase."

The man is actually a boy of about sixteen. He drags Karina's suitcase to their entrance door, gives her little boy a piece of candy, and tells Karina that he's looking for his father who's enlisted in the Territorial Defense, in other words, the militia. He wants to fight alongside his father—he can't keep hiding in the basement.

Yulia Leytes's grandmother has had enough of the basement. Yulia goes to her grandparents' apartment on Grushevsky Street, not far from the Verkhovna Rada. She wants to take them away with her. But her grandma says no, "I won't go anywhere and I'm not going to hide in the basement. I did it eighty years ago, when the Nazis occupied Kyiv. Do you really expect me to do that all over again? No, I can't do it anymore. Whatever happens, happens."

Save Yourself

From a state of desperate resignation to one of desperate selfishness is only a small step. Remember Alla Achasova's friends who promised to take her and her children away from Kharkiv in their car but then left without even telling her they were leaving? Well, this wasn't the only instance. People sit alone with their children inside four walls during the shelling. They don't feel any sympathy from those around them, nor do they receive any offers of help, so they decide: *Okay then, I won't help anyone either. I'll get out of here on my own.*

In Kharkiv, Zakhary B. talks to his wife Tatyana (who couldn't make bread) while their exhausted children sleep on the floor in the entryway. For some reason they've decided their deliverance can only come from the Russian side. This is supported by a chain of impeccable logic. The Russians will take the city, and then the shelling will stop. The Russians will take the whole country, and then there'll be peace. And if the Russian takeover of Kharkiv is delayed, then what they should do is obvious—flee to Russia. Salaries are higher in Russia. The cities there have lots of amenities and they're decorated with fantastic lights. In Russia, the state language is, obviously, Russian—which is Zakhary and Tatyana's mother tongue. They suddenly remember: Yes, there were cases of injustice. Russian-speaking citizens of Ukraine were required to fill out official papers in Ukrainian. Their children were required to study Ukrainian at school.

For several days Zakhary and Tatyana sit in the entryway of their apartment and wait for the Russians to take Kharkiv. But it doesn't happen right away, and the shelling continues. During the shelling, there are extremely long and extremely dangerous lines to get bread. But Zakhary comes up with a solution. He's a driver, and some of his colleagues now work on bread trucks—delivering bread, the most valuable commodity in the blockaded city. Following a centuries-long tradition of nepotism and corruption, they give bread to their family and friends, with a reasonable markup, before delivering the rest to the stores. Zakhary has enough bread for his family, but they need other food. Unfortunately for him, none of his relatives was delivering milk, canned goods, rice, or buckwheat.

They then decide to flee to Russia. Zakhary is most afraid of Ukrainian checkpoints, and so he comes up with a story. Even though he's traveling east, he's not trying to get to the Russian city of Belgorod; he's going to a village on Ukrainian territory where he has a house, a safe place for his children, with a cellar full of potatoes, pickled vegetables, and marinated meat. The Ukrainian soldiers let them through the checkpoints without any problems. They probably realize Zhakhary is lying, but they see three children inside the car and let them go. There are a lot of stories on Russian TV about Ukrainian soldiers detaining refugees, calling them traitors, and shooting at their cars. But Zhakhary passes through three Ukrainian checkpoints without a hitch.

They finally reach the first Russian checkpoint. Zakhary doesn't believe it. He suspects they're Ukrainian soldiers disguised as Russian soldiers to dupe Zakhary into revealing his pro-Russian views and then—he's a goner. They approach the car. The soldiers are wearing red armbands. The letter "Z" is written on the armored vehicle. Zakhary still doesn't believe it. He thinks it's an ambush, and now his plan of fleeing to Russia will be uncovered. But suddenly Zakhary sees that all the soldiers are wearing a black-and-orange St. George's ribbon in their buttonholes. This is a sure sign. Zakhary is certain that Ukranian soldiers couldn't bring themselves to wear a St. George's ribbon, even as a disguise, just like vampires can't wear an Orthodox cross or a garlic necklace. And when a soldier approaches his car, opens his mouth and starts asking questions, Zakhary relaxes completely—the soldier has a Russian accent. No Ukrainian could have such an accent.

Zakhary tells me his story on Russian territory, at a temporary accommodation center for refugees. His story is an exception. By my estimation, even on Russian territory, pro-Russian refugees like Zakhary make up less than ten percent. As a rule, people are grateful for a place to stay, for food and clothes, but they dream of returning home, and they begin their war stories with the statement: "You attacked us."

Making Sacrifices

In the refugees' conversations, more and more often I hear stories not about heroism but about small everyday acts of self-sacrifice. This is probably a primordial instinct—to sacrifice something in order to save yourself.

Yulia Leytes says goodbye to her grandma (probably forever—how much longer do her elderly grandparents have left?) and, wearing her trendy headphones, walks through her beloved Kyiv. She goes to her father's to ask if he wants to drive with her to the West. But her father refuses. He doesn't want to go, plus he no longer has any means of transportation. He gave his car to some friends who otherwise wouldn't have been able to take their children away from Kyiv. There it is, a sacrifice.

Victoria Svetlich leaves with her daughter, but she's very upset, in tears over leaving their vintage piano behind and, most importantly, her plants. Victoria's home is full of plants: orchids, lemons, and palms. She has a green thumb—everything she touches grows. She puts her plants in basins with water, but how long will their exile last? A month? A year? The rest of her life? In any of those scenarios, her plants will die. This is what Victoria thinks, but on the staircase, she runs into her neighbor who tells her to leave the plants on the staircase landing. This neighbor tells everyone in the building to put their plants on the staircase landing. She's not leaving and will water the plants as long as she's alive. A small everyday sacrifice.

After Karina Kovalchuk recovers from her cold, she takes her son and her huge suitcase and goes to the railroad station to travel first to her parents in Chernovtsy and from there to her husband in Romania. Of course, Karina packs vegetarian food for the road: apples, bread—she even manages to snag a few containers of yogurt.

The railway station is so overcrowded Karina can't make it onto the first train. Other trains aren't departing according to any schedule, not even the wartime schedule that appears on the Ukrainian railroad site every day at midnight. As Karina waits for a train, she gets acquainted with the young woman next to her who is sitting not on a suitcase but on a small gym bag—the only thing she had time to pack. This woman is a teacher from Chernigov who had left in such a hurry she now has neither money nor food, and she doesn't know what to do. As they wait, they chat for several hours until, finally, the arrival of a train to Chernovtsy is announced. Karina should run to get onto that train before it's completely packed. But before taking off she opens her suitcase and gives that woman all the food she has—apples, bread, yogurt—keeping nothing for herself, not even for her son. It will take more than a full day for the train to reach Chernovtsy. And for all that time Karina's neighbors in the train compartment will feed her. Did I say this was a small everyday sacrifice? But is this really a small sacrifice when a woman traveling alone into the unknown with her child gives all her food to a stranger?

Until the criminologists finish their work, little is known about the small town of Bucha—which became known throughout the world when hundreds of civilians perished under Russian occupation. But there's a moving story about a family trapped in the basement of a collapsed house. They were buried so deep under debris it would take a professional rescue team to get them out. But, as the story goes, one woman, probably a janitor or a groundskeeper, ignored the strict orders of the Russian military authorities not to leave their shelters and went every night to feed those people through the cracks between the concrete slabs.

I couldn't confirm this legend of the fearless groundskeeper. But if this brave, self-sacrificing woman really exists, then with this paragraph I petition that she be awarded the honorary title of Hero of Ukraine.

Begging for Mercy

In Bucha, among the many short and scattered testimonies of refugees collected by the independent online newspaper *The Insider*, one story stands out. It's an interview with a young woman named Kristina. Kristina recounts how one day she had to ask for help from some Russian soldiers, who by that time weren't predisposed to provide help to anyone. Such a day inevitably arrives. People's capacity to endure wears out. People leave their basements and approach the enemy soldiers—*Have some mercy, let us go, help us leave.* It's strange to ask the people who caused your misery for help, but there was simply no one else to ask.

Kristina leaves her basement and goes outside. On the street, there are corpses lying here and there. Kristina approaches the soldiers, possibly the same soldiers who killed these people, and asks if she can drive away with her small child. The soldiers say, "No, you can't leave by car. The soldiers will fire at any moving vehicle without warning. But you can walk."

Kristina puts her child in a stroller and makes her way through the corpses lying on the pavement. *Don't look back. Don't look around. Just push your stroller.*

Kristina passes through one checkpoint, a second checkpoint, then a third . . . As soon as she passes through the third checkpoint, a soldier yells to her from behind: "Stop!"

Kristina stops, raises her hands, and waits for a gunshot. But instead of shooting, the soldier says: "Go on."

Dozens of times different refugees have told me, independently, how soldiers let them go, didn't hurt them, or even helped them. This is how they tell their stories, but I think this is "survivor bias." If at the third checkpoint the soldiers had decided not to let Kristina go but to shoot her instead, she wouldn't have been able to tell us her story. The man on a bicycle who was killed in Bucha—the man whose photo was circulated by all the information agencies in the world—he can't tell us anything. That family that was shot in their car can't tell us anything either. And that's why the stories about the noble deeds of Russian soldiers we hear firsthand, from the refugees themselves. But the stories about atrocities are usually told through indirect evidence.

In Tsirkuny near Kharkiv, when Alyona Klyuchka runs out of food, she approaches a Russian officer who is standing with a rifle on her street. She approaches him and says that she doesn't have any food for her child. The officer calls over to his soldiers and asks them to share whatever they can from their dry rations. The soldiers share their food, and a minute later Alyona's arms are full of crackers, canned goods, and bread.

Then she asks if it's possible for her family—she, her husband, and their son—to leave somehow—they don't have a car. The officer promises that in a couple of days there will be an army rotation. A bus with fresh soldiers will arrive, and the tired ones, the ones who shared their food with Alyona, will be taken behind the frontline.

"I'll try to get you on that bus," the officer says. "Where do you live?"

Alyona points at her relative's house where they've been staying in the basement. Two days later the officer comes and knocks on the wall. The occupier says: "I'm sorry, I was mistaken: There will be no rotation." What kind of artillery school teaches its officers to treat civilians this way on occupied territory? He says: "I can only take you to the nearest checkpoint and there, I hope, the guys will be able to find room for you in the passing cars."

This officer does indeed take Alyona, her husband, and their son to the checkpoint. There are quite a few cars with refugees passing through, and some of them have a space for one person. The soldiers stop the cars, and the officer asks the drivers: "Can you take one more?"

First, they put the boy in a passing car, then the woman in another, and the man goes in a third. The officer returns to his weapon only after he's made sure that this family of refugees has left.

Of course, this is "survivor bias." Of course, enemy soldiers look noble in the stories told by those who survived and were rescued, while those who perished are silent.

But the fact remains: There is at least one artillery school in Russia where the cadets are taught to share their food with civilians, have mercy on refugees, and help women carry their suitcases.

Chapter 3
Escape

> "Beginning on March 4, humanitarian corridors are opened daily exclusively for humanitarian purposes in the direction of Kiev, Chernihiv, Sumy, Kharkov and Mariupol, from which one humanitarian corridor was opened to Russia and another, through territory controlled by Kiev, to the western border of Ukraine. Along all these routes Russian Armed Forces will observe a 'regime of silence,' despite the fact that this will slow the pace of the special military operation. This is being done for the sole purpose of sparing civilians." Official Telegram Channel of the Russian Ministry of Defense, March 25, 2022.

An Intersection in Bucha

Tanya K. sits in the car with her husband and seven-year-old daughter. The girl is strictly ordered to keep her eyes down and to look only at the floor. Tanya, too, tries not to look up. Their car has been standing still for five hours, since ten in the morning, and now it's three o'clock in the afternoon. The calendar shows March 9, 2022. All this time Tanya, her husband, and their daughter haven't had any food, any water, and haven't used a bathroom. The car is at an intersection. The intersection is in Bucha, a small town that will soon become known to the entire world as the place where four hundred civilians perished under the Russian occupation. There are cars everywhere—in front of their car, behind it, and on both sides—many, many cars. Tanya says there are about three thousand cars at that intersection. They're all waiting for the humanitarian corridor to be opened that will make it possible for them to leave the town. But the humanitarian corridor is still not opened. Tanya has only a vague idea of how humanitarian corridors are opened.

How exactly does it happen? Does a Russian traffic controller in military uniform show up and begin waving a small green flag? Or will it be a white flag? In any case, there are no traffic controllers, and there is no information about the opening of the humanitarian corridor. The column of tanks passes through the perpendicular street. About an hour later, the column returns. Or is it already a different tank column? Tanya doesn't know much about military vehicles or the insignias of the different Russian regiments. She tries to calm herself down thinking that if the troops are moving by tank, they're not mercenaries from the private Wagner Group nor are they Chechen special forces, known as Kadyrovtsy—who, as rumor has it, are particularly cruel to civilians.[3]

Tanya's family has now been living in occupied Bucha for fourteen days. In the first days, Tanya even tried to work, or more precisely, tried to go to the branch office she managed of a major insurance company. The office is located on Vokzalnaya Street. On the second day of the war, Tanya almost made it there. She turned the corner onto Vokzalnaya Street and froze: The street was covered with dead bodies. Russian soldiers and people in civilian clothes lay mixed together on the street. What happened here? What could all this mean? There were messages on social media that the Russians shelled the city even though their own troops had already entered it. Or was it the Ukrainian army that shelled the Russian military columns, and civilians got caught under the bombardment? Or did the Russians hide behind the civilians, who were thereby forced to accompany the Russians to their destruction? Tanya couldn't figure out what had happened on Vokzalnaya Street. For a minute, she

[3] Kadyrovtsy is the unofficial name for a paramilitary organization in Chechnya, Russia, that is nominally under the umbrella of the Russian National Guard. Made up mostly of ethnic Chechens, the Kadyrovtsy are named after Akhmad Kadyrov, the first president of the Chechen Republic, who defected to the Russian side during the Second Chechen War.

just stood there in a daze, then she turned around, ran home, and hasn't left her apartment for two weeks.

On the second day of the war the electricity was shut off and there was no water. On February 25, many people were leaving, and Tanya wanted to leave too. But Tanya's neighbors—two women and two children who had gotten in their car and driven off in the direction of Kyiv—returned in two hours, covered in dirt and blood. They said their car came under fire at a Russian checkpoint but, thank God, no one was seriously injured. They had to get out of the car and crawl through a field under the whistle of bullets, doing their best to make the children move faster but not stand up. They had to crawl most of the way home, occasionally running through the side streets. But there was no water at home for Tanya's neighbors to clean the cold March dirt off themselves and their children. Looking at them, Tanya got scared to leave.

The next day the city authorities announced there'd be an evacuation train leaving from the railway station. It was painful to even think of making their way again through Vokzalnaya Street. Especially with a child! How can you walk your daughter through a field of corpses? Should she blindfold her? It all was terrifying, but Tanya kept packing, until the city authorities announced that the evacuation train was full, they couldn't take anyone else, and asked civilians not to put themselves in danger by walking through the streets unless absolutely necessary. They promised one more evacuation train the next day, but the railway bridge was blown up that night, making further evacuations impossible.

At least they got their electricity back, and water was restored for a day and a half. Tanya managed to fill all the bottles, pots, and teapots she had at home with water. Then the gas was turned off. And the electricity. And the water again. It made no sense to go outside. All the stores in the city had been looted, so there was no food to be had. The pharmacies, too, had been looted. From her window, Tanya saw how the Russian soldiers herded people into the basement of the school across from her house. On social media, the people from that basement were posting that they'd been locked in, and that the only good news was that they hadn't been executed yet. Every day, there were testimonies on social media about executions on the streets.

Every day from two to three, the shelling would stop—the troops probably had their lunch break. From her window, Tanya saw how people walked out onto the streets during that hour—to feed their animals, check on their relatives, collect some spilled millet on the supermarket floor. Or get shot if a Russian soldier suspects you're a spy or an informant or if he thinks that packet of millet you're carrying is a bomb.

During this quiet time Tanya would walk inside her building. The tenants got organized, locked the front door, and took turns patrolling the entrance. It wasn't clear how those guards were supposed to stop soldiers in the event they decided to break in. The staircase landings became improvised markets for bartering. You couldn't buy anything for money anymore. They exchanged grain for sugar, canned meat for lard, or coffee for cigarettes. On the tenth day, a missile hit the apartment near Tanya's. The staircase bartering became much more reserved and cautious. People preferred to stay in their apartments and follow the two-wall rule—meaning, they would hide in their entryways where they were separated from the street by at least two walls. By the end of the third week, they stopped going out into the stairwell, even during the quiet hours—as there was nothing left to barter. The food had run out. The hungry days were here.

On March 9, one of the first of the hungry days, a neighbor knocked on Tanya's door and told her a green corridor for private cars would be opened soon. Tanya and her husband decided to leave. And they've now been waiting at the intersection for almost six hours, but the humanitarian corridor is still not open.

Tanya turns to comfort her daughter in the back seat—*Don't worry, sweetie, just don't look up, keep looking down.* As she turns around, she sees how the third and fourth cars behind them suddenly leave the column and drive toward the intersection in the oncoming lane. They cross the intersection and turn in the direction of Kyiv. Tanya closes her eyes and covers her ears. She waits for a shot from a grenade launcher or gun bursts. But no shots are fired. Tanya opens her eyes and sees that, following those first cars, more refugees are turning in the direction of Kyiv—a second car, then a third, and a fourth . . . The column begins moving. The cars that were in front of them have left, and the road is clear. The cars that were behind them are now driving around Tanya's car. Many cars are without windows or damaged by shrapnel. Almost all the cars are strewn with white sheets, pillowcases, or towels with the sign *Children*. "So, what are you waiting for? Let's go," Tanya says to her husband, and they start driving.

The column moves slowly. There are dead bodies on both sides of the road. *Don't look up, sweetie, look at the floor.* There is a Russian checkpoint in front of them, and the column stops. It's not clear whether the Russians received the order to open a humanitarian corridor or they simply see the three-thousand-car column and conclude that the corridor has been opened because people are coming. One way or the other, the soldiers let the column pass—one car at a time, after thoroughly searching through the photographs in the refugees' phones and throwing their sim cards into a ditch. They confiscate valuables like computers when they find them, otherwise they let the cars through. At a speed of one car every fifteen minutes, the column passes through four Russian checkpoints. By the time they make it through the last checkpoint, it's already nighttime. The column now stretches for ten or even fifteen kilometers.

They drive in the dark toward Kyiv when suddenly the sky above them bursts into flame, and an artillery battle begins.

Bombs, missiles, or multiple launch rocket systems—Tanya doesn't know the name of the deadly metal flying above them with thunder and sirens, but for sure this is not a humanitarian corridor. It doesn't make sense to stop, and it doesn't make sense to turn back, so the column continues under fire, God willing. *Don't look up, sweetie, look at the floor, cover your ears with your hands.* By the time Tanya's car reaches the first Ukrainian checkpoint, the shootout in the sky is over.

It's two o'clock at night. There's a curfew in Kyiv, so only those who have a place to stay or relatives in the city and can provide the exact address and phone number of their host are allowed to enter. The rest spend the night near the checkpoint in a big parking lot next to some black structure in the distance—Tanya can't see it in the dark—it could be a warehouse or a shopping center. People build fires right on the parking lot asphalt, and volunteers from Kyiv feed the people, some of whom haven't eaten anything since morning, others for several days.

The Boatman

It's a huge risk to flee the occupied territories. When Yelena Chepurnaya leaves Chernigov on the eleventh day of the war, the city is still controlled by the Ukrainian army, but the battle for the city has already begun. When there is a lull in the battle, the Ukrainian military opens the bridge and lets civilians cross, as many as can make it over before another shootout begins. When the fighting resumes, they close the bridge and the column of refugees remains, waiting for that battle, which is taking place very close by, to end. This is the battle for the bridge. After waiting for many hours under shelling, Yelena's family manages to cross the river. And three hours later, she reads on social media that the bridge was finally blown up—destroyed simultaneously by both armies. It seems the Russians and the Ukrainians alike wanted to erect an unpassable water barrier between their armies to give them a break from fighting.

That break didn't happen, and the fighting continues with the same intensity, but there is no longer a bridge in Chernigov. The evacuation road is closed. And at this moment, the boatman appears.

No one has ever seen that boatman, and no one knows his name. He works only in the dark of night. In Chernigov, there are eighty volunteers from Rubikus, the international organization that helps refugees flee the fighting in Ukraine. And among the eighty volunteers on duty, the boatman will speak with only one, whose calls he does not respond to right away and with whom he talks very evasively.

The boatman never reveals beforehand the time and place of his pickups, that is, when he's ready to take the refugees across the river. This mysterious man doesn't reveal anything ahead of time, not even their arrival point on the other side of the Desna River, where buses should pick up the refugees. Usually it happens this way: When the refugees are already in the boat, the boatman tells the volunteer where he'll deliver them. The volunteer gets in touch with the bus drivers, but they refuse to drive to the specified location because they heard the road is mined. The volunteer then calls the boatman back and asks him to change the destination point as it's too dangerous. The boatman refuses and as a rule just cancels the trip; he herds the refugees off his boat, and then disappears for several days. The refugees go back home and wait. In two or three days the boatman suddenly calls the volunteer and says that he has new departure and arrival points. And the operation begins again.

It's impossible to say for sure, but there's a rumor among the refugees that the boatman is somehow connected to the Ukrainian army. It's possible he's a Ukrainian military man himself. In any case, his boat is big enough to take thirty people on board—it's certainly more than a small fishing boat. Before each ride, the boatman tells the volunteer that he's made a deal with "the guys"—meaning the Ukrainian soldiers. But it's impossible to deal with the Russians, and so the boatman can't guarantee the Russians won't shell their boat as it moves in the dark through the black water at a very low speed to make as little noise as possible.

The boatman collects his fee of five hundred dollars from each of the refugees taken aboard. It's not hard to calculate that each ride brings him fifteen hundred dollars. Of course, this money isn't just for him. Most likely "dealing with the guys" means bribing the soldiers to allow the slow-moving river boat to depart into the darkness. It's likely the Russian military shells the boat not because they want to kill the refugees but because they want the boatman to bribe them too. But the boatman is too stingy and would rather take the risk than pay too much; unlike Vovan (whose story is coming up), he probably can't reach an agreement with the Russian officers.

Most likely he's just too stingy. In the same way some airlines sell more tickets than there are seats on the plane in the hope that some passengers won't show up but the plane will still be full, the boatman signs up more people for each ride than he can possibly take aboard. Every time there are people left on the shore, the boat is always completely full, and the boatman pockets fifteen thousand dollars.

At night, on the dark water, without a single light on either shore, the big black boat moves slowly across the river. There are old people, children, and women in the boat. At the point of arrival, they hesitate. They're afraid to get off the boat as there isn't any pier. The boatman hurries them, and the people clumsily climb over the forward bow and slip into the icy water—some up to their knees, others up to their ankles. Then through the slippery mud they climb onto the shore where the buses are waiting for them. They are small buses, which no one in Ukraine has seen before.

As soon as the refugees are in their seats, the buses take off. They drive in the dark with their lights off. After driving no more than a kilometer they come under fire—several machine guns are firing at the same time. The bullets hit the sides of the bus and the windows, but the buses keep driving. They drive faster and faster—as fast as possible while traveling down those dark roads with their lights off. Finally, they make it past the gunfire. Was anyone killed? Is anyone injured? No, not this time, thank God. Those small buses are armored military vehicles.

82 Buses

One very rich Israeli bought those armored buses to rescue refugees from the war zone. He doesn't reveal his name but doesn't hide his Ukrainian origins. At least that's what Shimon Shlevich tells us. He's one of the founders of the Israel4Ukraine volunteer organization.

Shimon is a living illustration of the ironic saying about "Jewish luck." On February 23, 2022, he boarded a plane in Tbilisi to fly to Tel-Aviv with a layover in Kyiv, where he decided to spend a couple of days seeing friends. The next morning, he woke up to the sound of explosions—and with a now totally useless ticket from Boryspil airport to Ben-Gurion. Unlike native Kyivites, who were kept there by the houses, families, and unfinished business, Shimon wasn't planning to stay in a country at war and tried to get back home to Israel—a country that's fighting too but less intensely at that time than Ukraine. It took him two days to find a tourist agency prepared to send buses from Kyiv to Lviv. Shimon's Israeli experience helped him figure out that there are intercity buses even in countries at war.

It's just that the prices had skyrocketed because of the fighting. In late February and early March, renting a fifty-seat bus from Kyiv to Lviv could cost you ten thousand dollars. By the end of March, however, the price had dropped twofold—people had begun adjusting to the war.

In addition to Shimon, there are thirty people on that bus, people who by chance found themselves in the middle of a war. Without fail, they were stopped at every checkpoint. The Ukrainian guards suspected every man to be, if not a spy, then definitely a deserter. But as soon as the guards saw Israeli or European passports, they were let through. Renting a bus from Lviv to the Polish border was much easier, and it was a piece of cake to get from Poland to Israel.

While in Kyiv and then on his journey from the city, many friends from around the world were helping Shimon remotely: sending him road maps, finding the checkpoints with the shortest lines, recommending motels, and helping with paperwork and plane tickets. Finally, they started transferring money or offering to do so.

By the end of his journey, Shimon had created a network of people made up of his fellow travelers and his virtual friends, who had learned how to organize transfers anywhere in wartime Ukraine. In addition, they all had personal experience of Ukrainian roads, checkpoints, and border crossings.

After returning home and then moving to London, Shimon and his friends organized a transport company to provide Ukrainian refugees with semi-regular transportation to the West. The company's fleet now has eighty-two buses traveling from Kyiv, Dnipro, and Zaporizhzhia. On the buses, volunteers ask the refugees to donate whatever they can, but it's a pittance. So, they have to find the money to operate Israel4Ukraine. They start with those friends who called Shimon to offer their financial help on the first day of the war. Thousands of people make small donations, while a small number of people donate thousands of dollars. In the Israel4Ukraine call center, day and night more than a hundred operators spread out all over the world answer calls and requests for help. Their buses carry people from Ukraine and go back filled with humanitarian cargo—baby food, canned goods, or, for instance, drinkable water for the town of Mykolaiv, where the plumbing is destroyed. In the first month and a half, Shimon and his friends organized the evacuation of thirty-five hundred people. They were already thinking of gradually ramping up their activity when they noticed the stream of refugees was getting smaller, but then the second phase of the war—"the battle for the Donbas"—began, and the stream of refugees increased once again.

The hundreds of people evacuated by Israel4Ukraine constitute less than one percent of all Ukrainian refugees. Most of them leave on their own or use the evacuation trains and buses provided by the government and by international humanitarian organizations like the Red Cross, but bureaucrats are not flexible, and if something goes wrong, they just stop or cancel the entire convoy. Incidentally, there are already hundreds of volunteer organizations like the one created by Shimon and his friends, and their role in evacuating refugees is significant.

Israel4Ukraine's greatest innovation is, perhaps, an online form for refugees. All you need to do is fill it out and help is on the way. The Israeli businessman Alex Gurevich created the form, which consists of only three questions: your name, the number of family members, and your phone number. For people under shelling, for people whose hands are shaking from fear, insomnia, hunger, and cold—it's hard to answer even the simplest questions. So, it's just your name, the number of family members, and your phone number. Somewhere in Israel, Britain, Australia, or Canada, the call-center operators will call, and the mere fact of that call brings hope—someone is thinking about you somewhere on the other side of the world. The operators will ask about your particular circumstances, give instructions, indicate the time and place of the next evacuation, and try to provide some comfort. The operators will call again during the evacuation to see if everything is going according to plan and, if necessary, they'll modify the plan. The refugees, too, can call the operator at any time and ask any questions—and the refugees do call. Shimon relates that if the refugees on a bus traveling along the dark roads of the Chernihiv, Kyiv, or Galicia regions urgently need to use a bathroom, as a rule they won't tell the driver; they'll telephone their call-center operator in another part of the world, and that operator will call the driver and ask him to make a sanitary stop.

Vovan

Another important difference between volunteer-organized evacuations of refugees and official evacuations organized by the state and the Red Cross is that bureaucrats don't know how to rescue people from hot spots—from occupied Chernihiv or bombed out Mariupol. Only volunteers can do that; they can even evacuate people across a frontline.

It takes weeks for Irina Veryeschuk, the vice president of Ukraine, to arrange the opening of green corridors for refugees. She negotiates on the governmental level and talks with the United Nations, alternately pleading and cajoling. But one out of three times, something unforeseen happens—ranging from an exchange of gunfire to simple treachery—and the humanitarian corridor gets closed even before it was opened.

Church leaders organize a religious procession and under the cover of that procession take women and children from the ruins of the Azov steel plant, this citadel of Mariupol that kept fighting even after the entire city had been occupied. But it seems that God is not that omnipotent anymore, and the procession was canceled.

At this moment, Vovan appears.[4]

A man calling himself Vovan sent his photo to the Rubikus coordinator responsible for the evacuation of the refugees, explaining that he wanted to become a volunteer-driver to transport people away from hot spots. The Rubikus coordinator recoiled. Staring back at her from the computer screen was the face of a typical thug. A once broken now crooked nose, puffy eyes that looked with defiance at the camera, thin merciless lips that stretched into a sarcastic smile revealing missing teeth—an outlaw right out of central casting. The coordinator, however, didn't refuse the offer. Vovan took two hundred dollars for gas, wrote down the names and addresses of the old people who needed to be evacuated, and disappeared without a trace. The coordinator didn't lament the lost money for long—silly her, she shouldn't have trusted this gangster. But one week later, he emerged from the gunfire and returned with the elderly refugees. Moreover, the Rubikus volunteers couldn't praise Vovan enough; they kept saying, "Volodenka is such a good guy, he's so good, so wonderful!"

Alex Gurevich says that everywhere, literally in any of the hot spots—in Chernihiv, Mariupol, or Rubezhnoye—you can find a daredevil like Vovan. The only problem is figuring out somehow over the phone or through social media if the guy is a swindler. Alex even tried to make a list of the characteristics that might differentiate honest daredevils from con artists, but nothing came of it.

If an unknown driver calls and says he can evacuate five people from a city that's under attack, like Mariupol, for five hundred dollars per person, does it mean he's a swindler? It's possible, but Israel4Ukraine knows several examples of successful

---

[4] Vovan is a low colloquial form of the Russian name Vladimir. A more standard diminutive form is Volodya from which the affectionate diminutive Volodenka is formed. The latter is used below by the Rubikus volunteer Rita.

evacuations of that kind. One of them even happened in a refrigerator truck, where the refugees literally traveled inside the refrigerator until they reached Zaporizhzhia.

If a driver asks only for gas money and doesn't expect any compensation for his services, does it mean we're dealing with a selfless philanthropist and a patriot? No, it doesn't mean anything. In those areas caught up in the war, gas becomes a valuable commodity. If a swindler fills up five gas canisters in Zaporizhzhia, he can drive them through checkpoints, sell the gas for five, or even ten, times the price, and disappear. Or he can come back and say that he didn't find the refugees at the address given and then ask to be sent on another expedition. A driver can also tell stories about bribing Russian soldiers at the checkpoints when he's taking people from Kherson through the frontline. But the Russian soldiers aren't going to give you a receipt, so all you can do is believe that the driver bribed the Russian soldiers and didn't just pocket the money.

When daredevil drivers go on rescue missions, they never drive empty vehicles; they take along humanitarian aid—potable water, canned goods, soap, grains, and medications. And how can you verify a daredevil's claim that Russian soldiers took some of the humanitarian aid? And even if the driver sends you a video of civilians unloading boxes of food from his truck, how do you know who those people are? Are they really civilians living in the basements of Mariupol or are they the driver's relatives? Or just fakes?

This is a war, and you can't verify anything. During times of war the rules of financial accountability are turned upside down. It's well-known that if you deliver humanitarian aid in the form of medications, for example, you should, under no circumstances, carry any documents indicating how much that medication costs. If they're expensive, the checkpoint soldiers will demand money, justifying this highway robbery by saying, "Wow, they're expensive! So, you need to pay tax."

The only reliable way to evaluate a driver's honesty is to believe him, give him the money, and wait to see if he returns with the refugees. If he does come back with the refugees and wants to go on another run, and recommends his relative as a new driver, it would make sense to trust this daredevil and his relative. If a driver comes back with refugees five times but disappears on the sixth run, don't assume right away that he's a crook—he may have died. But he may have also gotten tired, then gave up, pocketed the money, and disappeared into the fog of war.

In any case, I can imagine a monument in the middle of the Taurian steppe—a minibus riddled by bullets with Vovan, Tolyan, Petro, or Vasil behind the wheel. They drive refugees. These amazing daredevils rescue people, and who are we to judge whether they do it out of reckless greed or selflessness.

A Place in Line

In general, it's hard to compare human behavior and human actions during war with how people behave in peace time. Within the span of a minute, the same person can show both self-sacrifice and baseness, and then baseness again, and after that self-sacrifice. In a flash, evil can turn out to be good, and good can turn out to be evil. Your impression of a person can be based entirely on how far, up to what episode, you listened to their story.

Take Karina Kovalchuk. At the railway station in Kyiv, she hears an announcement for the train to Lviv. On a sudden impulse, she gives all her food to a stranger, grabs her five-year-old son, and takes off—dragging her enormous suitcase behind her.

The crowd around her grows more and more dense. Karina can no longer walk by herself; all she can do is try to remain upright and not to fall, not to lose her son and her suitcase in the stream of human bodies. And this stream carries her toward the train.

This human stream crashes against the train like a wave crashing against the rocks, leaping forward and rolling back. There are no police officers there to regulate the human stream. Some girls in uniforms try in vain to organize the crowd. Not losing your child and your suitcase on the platform is as difficult as not losing them in the surf. Now the crowd surges, several people squeeze into a train car, but then a heavy woman falls off the steps and the human tide drags Karina backward. "Easy! Easy! A woman was crushed!"

The crowd surges once again and carries Karina back to the train. "Watch your suitcase, lady! Carry it the right way! You ruined my stockings!" With the third or fourth wave, Karina and her son are thrown into the train car, but at the last moment our skinny vegetarian doesn't have the strength to hold on to her suitcase, and it slips out of her hand. The suitcase falls, people trip over it, and walk over Karina's remaining possessions.

"My suitcase! My suitcase!" Karina yells. "Pass me my suitcase, please!"

A stranger hears her, lifts the suitcase, and . . . walks away from the train. He stole it! And there is nothing she can do about it. You're not going to leave an evacuation train to save your suitcase. The man with Karina's suitcase walks farther away. He stole it! Or maybe not? Maybe he's not leaving but was carried away by the surging crowd? The next moment, the human wave rolls over the train. The man lifts the suitcase high above his head and like a ball into a basketball hoop, he throws Karina's belongings into the vestibule.

"Here's your suitcase, young lady! Hold on to it! And take care of your kid!"

Only when her suitcase is inside the train does Karina realize that it's a crime against all the people left on the platform to have a suitcase with her. This suitcase takes up space. Instead of her suitcase another human being could have been evacuated.

It's crowded and dark inside the train. People share their food with Karina and her son. In the dark, Karina tries to figure out from its smell if the food she's being offered is vegetarian or not. Just in case, she barely eats anything and only feeds her son.

The train stops at a small dark station, the doors open, and two huge bags move into the vestibule, where there's plenty of luggage as it is and people sitting on those pieces of luggage.

"Step aside! Step aside!" an energetic woman screams and pushes her bags further inside the train. "Let me put my bags down!"

Then the loud woman opens her enormous bags and takes out sandwiches lovingly wrapped in paper, apples that had been washed and thoughtfully put into plastic bags, and small bottles of fruit juice.

"Pass it along! Pass it along!"

And she keeps passing along the food until both her bags are empty. She takes the empty bags under her arm and leaves the train even before the dumbfounded refugees have time to come to their senses and thank her or to ask if she feeds people out of goodwill or because she works for a charitable organization.

Almost all refugees have a story about strangers that fed them. Almost all of them talk about strangers who sheltered them for at least one night. But it doesn't mean that refugees don't have stories about how they were cheated or about a hysterical woman who tried to kick them out of line at the border.

Marina Polishchuk with her children and fiancé are leaving Kyiv in two cars and driving through Ternopil and Lviv. Marina takes her daughters, and her fiancé takes his former family—his ex-wife and their child. Marina manages to cover the six-hundred-kilometer distance to Lviv in only thirty-three hours. Then from Lviv Marina drives her car through Ivano-Frankivsk to the village of Yavorov where people she barely knows let her and her children stay overnight. In this village two days later, Russian missiles will fall on the military training grounds. Marina is exhausted and needs to get some sleep. The next day, Marina's fiancé gets up earlier to secure a spot for Marina in the line at the Shehyni-Medyka border checkpoint.

After a good night's sleep, Marina puts her children in the car and drives off. The line stretches for many kilometers. Many people, even those who are elderly or with children, walk to the checkpoint. Marina drives along the line and every minute or so someone asks who gave her the right to drive to the border ignoring the line. She calmly answers that her boyfriend got up early in the morning to save her a spot and after she takes his spot in line, he'll return to Kyiv in his car because, as you all know, there is martial law and men aren't allowed to leave the country. It works but only up to a point.

After Marina has gone about two kilometers along the line, a woman throws herself on the hood and pounds on it with her fists:

"Where are you going? Get out of here! The line is for everybody. Turn around, bitch!"

Marina again explains that her fiancé has been in line since early morning. It has no effect. Marina again explains that, obviously, her fiancé won't be able to cross the border anyway, and he'll drive back and give his spot to Marina. Again, no effect. Marina calls her fiancé and complains. He asks her to put the woman lying across the hood on the phone.

"Listen," he says in a voice that can't be countermanded. "Let her go. She'll take my spot in the line, and while she's waiting, I'll drive back and forth giving rides to old people, children, and pregnant women who are walking to the border."

In other words, Marina's fiancé tells the woman blocking

Marina's car that he'll help another hundred people skip the line. But for some paradoxical reason, the woman gets off the hood of the car and says to Marina: "Go."

Even after taking her fiancé's spot, Marina waits in line for twelve more hours. She has a lot of food—in Ternopil her grandmother made tons of blintzes and cutlets for them. Toilets are anywhere you like. To relieve themselves, people go a few meters away from their cars and squat in the reeds trying to ignore one other. The line moves slowly, very slowly. And all this time Marina's fiancé drives back and forth along the line to brings pedestrians, more than a hundred people, to the checkpoint. And no one in the line protests. Everyone sees what he's doing as a good deed.

Finally, Marina reaches the checkpoint. For the last time, her fiancé brings a woman with children. Marina steps out of her car, and so does her fiancé. They hug and kiss each other. Here is another idea for a war monument: a man and a woman standing in the middle of the road at the Shehyni checkpoint. They stand and hug each other. God only knows how long they'll be apart. A moment later, he'll return home to sign up for the Territorial Defense Forces and she'll cross the border with their children and enter a refugee camp.

Chapter 4
Shelter

> "The Ukrainian army continues systematic shelling of humanitarian convoys and attempts to shift responsibility for their inhuman acts onto divisions of Russian troops. During this week alone, 17 attacks on civilians traveling along humanitarian corridors were recorded." Official Telegram Channel of the Russian Ministry of Defense, March 25, 2022.

Triaging Refugees

The flap of a big, warm tent opens, and a young woman walks outside. She's dressed like all Southerners dress in colder climates—too warm, although it's almost spring here, in Poland. Wearing a down coat, a hat, and heavy, lined boots, the woman walks through the slush passing the other tents that have been set up along the road leading to the checkpoint on the Ukrainian border.

As strange as it may seem, a refugee camp looks a bit like a fairground, only without the music or people with carefree, happy faces. But there's smoke coming out of braziers where the Spaniards are cooking paella in huge pans, and there are the Hungarians stirring goulash with a Rabelaisian-size ladle in a ten-bucket kettle. The Germans fry sausages and feed their compatriots—German psychologists who came to help the refugees but didn't find enough translators now languish without anything to do.

This is Medyka, a small Polish town on the border and a primary accommodation camp for refugees, where the people fleeing Ukraine are admitted, provided with first aid, and sorted. In military field medicine a key step is the triage of the injured—so it is with the admission of refugees.

Our Israeli volunteer—a young woman from the Israel Psychological Association—crosses the border without showing any documents. She crosses the border at least twenty times a day, and all the border patrol officers recognize her. Before they can give her a smile or a greeting or make some politically incorrect joke about her Southern beauty, she's already walking along the line of cars and pedestrians that stretches to the border from the Ukrainian side.

The woman looks around attentively. She sees an almost brand-new car with a mother and two teenage children inside—they can wait. Then she spots a bus, a PAZ model from Soviet times; it's cold inside and not very comfortable, but the passengers are rather young—they too can wait. Now she catches a glimpse of a woman with an infant—she's standing in the March drizzle looking completely lost.

"Come with me."

"Me? Where?"

And there's a heavy elderly woman whose legs are swollen; she can barely walk. She's dragging a chair behind her. It would be interesting to know how long she's been carrying it. Has it come all the way from Chernigov? From Sumy? From Zaporizhzhia? This woman walks about twenty steps then sits on her chair and rests. She gets up, stumbles another twenty steps, and rests again.

"Come with me."

"Me? Where?"

And then there's a woman with a girl of about ten. At first glance the woman looks like she's okay, but the trained eye of our Israeli psychologist sees that there's something seriously wrong with this woman—she's holding her daughter's hand so tightly the girl's fingers are turning blue. It clearly hurts, but the girl tries to endure the pain, knowing from experience that if she tries to free her hand, it will only make things worse.

"Come with me."

"Me? Where?"

"I'll take you across the border without waiting."

After recognizing signs of complete exhaustion in these five people, the psychologist takes them through the border checkpoint with only a cursory examination of their passports. Then she brings them into her tent where Vika Lagodinskaya is already waiting for them. She's the one who has recounted all this to me.

Vika is a volunteer. She's a little bit of an amateur psychologist, but mainly she's a translator. She's Jewish, was born in Russia, and now has an IT company in London. Many of her computer programmers work remotely from Ukraine, so the refugees' problem is close to Vika's heart. She signed up as a volunteer through the Israel Psychiatric Association, and this was a good decision—they put her on the schedule and told her when to arrive to replace the translator who worked here before her. In general, you can come to a refugee camp as a volunteer without making prior arrangements. That's what, for example, the Spaniards did: They just showed up in Medyka with their grills, pans, and spices for paella. They registered, got their badges, and now they feed everyone with paella. But then again, without any prior arrangements you might find yourself in the situation of the German psychologists who arrived to find that there were no translators for them. All they can do is loiter around the camp and eat their sausages.

Vika bought a ticket to Kraków, and, with her friend and fellow psychologist, she sublet an apartment near Medyka through Airbnb, rented a car in Kraków, and set off. When she was only a few kilometers from Medyka, she got lost in a forest and knocked on the door of a small hut. A man in his underwear opened the door and pointed—the border's over there. And now Vika is sitting in the Israeli tent with the five refugees, women ranging in age from seven to seventy.

As soon as the woman with the infant enters the tent, she

sits on the floor and falls asleep, relaxed by the warm air. You shouldn't sit on the floor—it feels like the tent is warm, but the only thing that's warm is the air pushed in by the powerful ventilators. The tent is on the ground, and the ground is still cold. Vika wants to offer the young woman a blanket to put on the floor, but the elderly woman brings her chair closer to Vika's desk.

"What happened to your legs?"

"It's just ulcers."

"What kind of ulcers?"

"From diabetes," the woman pulls down her wool stocking and shows Vika her swollen legs covered with diabetic ulcers; it's almost gangrene.

"Diabetes?!"

"But everyone has diabetes," the old woman answers, unperturbed.

"What are you taking?"

"Just herbs, nothing special."

Vika will see many similar cases of extreme neglect of chronic illnesses among refugees from the Ukrainian provinces. Hypertension, diabetes, and cancer haven't been treated at all. It's clear to Vika what she has to do with these people—send them to the medical tent.

Meanwhile the woman on the floor has fainted, or she might be in a deep sleep. As she sleeps, she holds her infant tight and shakes from the cold that's already gotten into her bones. Vika gets up, walks toward the woman, and touches her shoulder, "Wake up, wake up, you'll freeze to death." She tries very carefully to take the infant, but even in sleep, the woman holds her baby with an iron grip and mutters something in a language Vika doesn't recognize. Could it be Romani, even though the woman doesn't look like a Roma? Vika finally manages to wake the mother up and take her behind the screen; she gives her a mug of hot coffee and a bottle with formula for the baby—in such a state of exhaustion, she probably doesn't have any breast milk. Sitting on the couch behind the screen, the woman holds her baby with her left hand and the bottle with her right, so the child can eat while she sleeps. It won't be easy to help her. You can't just send her to a temporary accommodation camp, putting her on a bus taking refugees somewhere in the middle of the country. The volunteer driver will need to be attentive and caring and take her directly to a nice host family or to a women's crisis center. Vika will look for such a driver, such a family, and such a center in the volunteer chat rooms, and she will of course find them. But for now, the woman needs to get some sleep, at least fifteen minutes, and then Vika will ask her some questions—does she have relatives anywhere, maybe a sister in Prague or a cousin in Cyprus? If so, Vika will find a volunteer charter flight to Cyprus, and an attentive driver will take this woman to the airport and leave her in the caring hands of the flight attendants.

But Vika has forgotten about the third woman. She's still standing near the entrance to the tent and squeezing her ten-year-old daughter's hand, which is now almost completely blue.

"Come in," Vika smiles. "Have a seat. I'll try to help you."

"I really need to use a bathroom," the woman says quietly, as if embarrassed, and with such desperation as if she's been waiting for a thousand years.

"Yes, of course, it's over there," Vika points the woman in the direction of the latrines.

But the woman doesn't move: "I can't leave my child."

"Don't worry, I'll keep an eye on her. What's your name?"

But the woman doesn't move:

"Hold her hand. Do you promise to hold her hand the entire time I'm gone? I'll be quick, two minutes. Do you promise?"

"Yes, of course, no problem," Vika says sweetly, then takes the girl's hand, and leads her to a chair. "Have a seat. What's your name?"

The woman takes a few slow steps toward the exit and disappears behind the flap that separates the warm air inside the tent from the cold air outside. But a moment later she's back.

"You're not holding her! You're not holding her! Always hold her hand, you promised! Two minutes! Can't you hold her hand for two minutes?" The girl obediently puts her crumpled fingers into Vika's palm, gently tapping it with her fingertips—a secret sign, a conspiratorial handshake. As if to say, *Can't you see, Mom isn't herself. Just do what she says and don't argue.*

Oddly enough, this case is rather straightforward. The woman and her daughter will recover soon enough—this isn't physical exhaustion; they're just very scared. What's more, this woman left her eighteen-year-old son in Ukraine, where martial law doesn't allow him to leave, and this makes her cling even more tightly to her daughter. But these worries will subside. After they've spent a couple of days in safety, the mother and daughter will be able to join one of the streams of refugees that will somehow bring them to a more or less acceptable placement and provide them with social assistance.

When the woman comes back from the bathroom, Vika passes the girl's fingers into her mother's hand without losing contact for even a second. Then she puts these poor things on the bus that will take them to a humanitarian center nearby.

The Humanitarian Center

The shopping mall in Medyka, or more precisely in Przemyśl, has been transformed into a humanitarian center. They say that in Polish cities the shopping centers were closed even before the war because of the COVID-19 pandemic. In place of the smaller signs for Zara, Uniqlo or even Christian Dior, there is now one big sign—Humanitarian Center.

Somehow, this society of addicted consumers was seamlessly

transformed into a society where people see helping others as their main purpose in life. The consumerist society described in millions of economic studies and considered the cornerstone of prosperity has ceased to exist. But the Nobel Prize winners in economics have yet to write any serious research papers about societies based on humanitarian assistance. How does such a society function? The goods that are redistributed in the humanitarian centers, where do they come from? How do you explain the inequality? Why is one person living in a former shopping center welcomed by a successful Dutch lawyer into his house in Mallorca, while another will have to do with just a bed in a room for six in a hostel on the outskirts of Poznań? It's obvious that for some the bitter taste of emigration will stay with them, while for others, becoming a refugee will turn out to be the beginning of a new, better life. How does it all work? What's the difference between the right emigration strategy and the wrong one? What place determines whether emigration will become the launching pad for future success in life or the determinant of future failure?

I believe that place is here, in the humanitarian center.

There are guards at the entrance. Anyone can walk into the tents at the border, but to enter the humanitarian centers, you must be a registered refugee or a volunteer.

So, here is the first rule for refugees: register. Just as the price of any art object depends on its provenance—its origin and sales history—a successful refugee placement depends on their registration records—the unbroken chain of registrations from a half-collapsed basement in Chernigov or Mariupol to a decent accommodation and a job in Cologne or Barcelona.

Many people, especially those who are strong, young, and well-off, rely too much on themselves and disregard the registration formalities. Yulia Leytes, for example, ignored them. She left Kyiv driving an expensive car with her dependable, wealthy friends. She jokingly called herself a VIP-refugee and refused any help. And what happened? She got stuck in Belgrade because she hadn't asked anyone about the rules for taking animals across the border and so had to waste a lot of time registering her dog named Odesa. The veterinarian there kept delaying the dog's registration and kept talking about the Nazis that had assumed power in Ukraine and about the Odesa nationalists who had mistreated him, a Serbian, when he used to visit Odesa. All this chatter and duplicity weren't fatal, but they were humiliating.

Every night beds are set up on the sales floor of the former shopping center. During the day, all the beds are taken away—to change the bedding and to disinfect the blankets, pillows, mattresses, and the entire space. The Polish army takes care of it. The practical reason for setting up the beds every night and disassembling them in the morning is to avoid epidemics. The authorities are afraid of lice, scabies, typhus, cholera, and of course Covid.

But there's also a symbolic reason behind the practice—to prevent the refugees from idling. We'll see later that, in Russia, as a rule, nothing is done to help the refugees become independent. Only the most determined people will take charge of their lives; most lie around all day long doing nothing. They play with their phones, read the news, but don't even try to improve their situation—they just wait.

Taking the beds away every morning makes the refugees get up and go somewhere—to the bank, the passport office, the railroad station, the unemployment center, or to church—it doesn't matter where, the main thing is not to lie around.

I've read that some Egyptologists believe the hieroglyphs on the inner walls of ancient sarcophagi are in essence calls to action, motivation for the dead: "Wake up! You aren't dead! Get up! Go and introduce yourself to the gods! It's high time you began your afterlife, or you'll risk remaining an embalmed log for all eternity."

I don't know if that's correct in regard to Ancient Egypt, but it's certainly true for refugees, and hence the second rule for refugees: Don't lie around during the day! Do something while all the offices are open. You must begin your afterlife for there's no returning to your former one.

In reality, when the beds in the humanitarian center have been taken away and the refugees can't lie around anymore, the women (most people there, of course, are women and children) go outside, but only for a smoke. They stand around, browse through pictures on their phones, and show one another images of themselves from before the war, in beautiful dresses, holding bouquets of flowers, with laughing children on carnival rides, with men who stayed in Ukraine to fight or are waiting to be called up. "Girls, has any of you brought even one nice dress?" They learn that no one brought any dresses. Only one refugee, Maryana, brought rollers. Every morning Maryana shows up with beautiful curls. From time to time, other women ask Maryana if they can just hold her rollers in their hands. These rollers are like a symbol for them, evidence of a past life they cannot return to. However, very few refugees truly grasp this.

There's a children's room and booths in the humanitarian center that are open from early morning. Some of the booths represent countries that are accepting refugees or transportation companies, while some booths give away clothes. For a refugee, clothes are very important, and here comes the third rule: Take good care of yourself. It's very important to wash your face, shave, brush your teeth, comb your hair, and dress well. Subconsciously, people, including government bureaucrats, are more willing to help people who look good—it's easier to relate to a person in clean clothes than to someone in rags. So Maryana is right to curl her hair and put on makeup every morning, although she hasn't figured out yet where she will go next.

There are many opportunities at the transportation company booths—buses to Western Poland, buses to the Czech

Republic, buses to Germany. Trains go all over Europe, and there's free passage for Ukrainian refugees, at least there was during the first three months of the war. The only problem is that most buses and trains don't allow animals.

Katya L., a volunteer from the humanitarian center in Vienna, says that in her experience, every fourth refugee family has brought a pet—a dog, a cat, a chinchilla, a hamster, a turtle, and so on. An elderly man with his daughter (maybe even his granddaughter) comes to her desk. The girl has a cat carrier on her lap. The man asks:

"Can you tell me if there's a litter box in the humanitarian center? You know we have a pure-bred cat, with an excellent pedigree, who can go only in a litter box and nowhere else. He's holding it for now, you understand?"

There is a litter box in the humanitarian center. Katya takes them to the pet area corner, and the cat is let go. The poor animal doesn't even look around; he doesn't sniff anything or sneak around like cats usually do; it runs straight to the litter box and defecates. Katya says that she's never seen such a distinct expression of happiness and relief on a cat's face!

That's the problem. Pets have ways of expressing their emotions, and so we sympathize with them.

The fourth immutable rule for refugees—no pets! Children help a refugee find a placement, while animals only hinder the process. It would've been more sensible to put them to sleep than to drag them along, but few people are capable of doing that. Most people take their dogs and cats with them, even when they're running away from missile attacks. Some people can't find decent accommodations because of their pets and wander from one humanitarian center to another. Many have even stayed in the war zone with their pets. And some have perished.

Evgeny Pinelis, a medical doctor from the US who used to work in Przemyśl, tells me about one veterinarian from Kharkiv who arrived at the humanitarian center with twenty pythons. His wife came the next morning with twenty more pythons. Those forty pythons lived in Dr. Pinelis's tiny room behind the pharmacy. And every day the vet would show the pythons to anyone who wanted to see them; he'd let children hold the pythons and would give long talks about their traits and behaviors. Some lectures lasted several hours and were full of the most interesting facts about the lives of pythons. In his free time the veterinarian would check out the booths of the various countries and try to figure out the best place for his pythons to live—note, not the best place for people to live! He finally figured it out—Australia. And then the volunteers from the booths of all the transportation companies tried to figure out how to relocate forty enormous snakes from Przemyśl to Sydney.

The main purpose of the country booths is to give refugees enough information to make an informed decision—what country would fit them best. Most Ukrainian refugees, however, have never been abroad, don't know a foreign language, and have a rather vague idea how the rest of the world operates.

At the country booths and the psychologists' tables, volunteers try to convince refugees to make sensible decisions about where to relocate. But these decisions aren't always sensible.

Consider, for example, the middle-aged woman from a small village who suffers from a number of chronic diseases. She receives an offer to go to a German farm—it's a familiar environment, there are good welfare benefits for people in her age group, and she'll live in a separate guest house. But no, she's got it into her head that she needs to live in a big city because that's where doctors and hospitals are and she's in dire need of medical help. And there's no way to convince her that the hospitals in German villages are no worse than the hospitals in the capital. The result: Instead of relaxing on a farm in her own guest house, she now lives in a Hamburg hostel in a room for two.

Or another woman, young and excitable, who has dreamed

her whole life about seeing Paris. She refuses to go to any other French city. The result: she lives in a hostel on the outskirts of the French capital, in a neighborhood with a high crime rate. She still hasn't seen the Champs-Élysées, Montmartre, or the Louvre.

Despite all the efforts of the psychologists and volunteers in the humanitarian centers, many refugees make mistakes in choosing the country of their placement. So, the fifth important rule for refugees, a rule that needs to be followed before war breaks out: travel. Try to see the world, take note of different customs, and make new acquaintances. Who knows, maybe tomorrow, when your country is being bombed, these strangers will give you shelter.

The Hosts

The people who host immigrants are a strange breed. In volunteer organizations, people who are ready to take refugees into their homes are called hosts. Apart from basic human compassion, these hosts are driven by another remarkable feeling—that of belonging to a community where it's the norm to offer people in trouble a place in your own home.

Yuri and Karina Kovalchuk find their hosts by chance. When it comes to the five ground rules for refugees mentioned above, Yuri and Karina broke them all. We remember that Karina gave all her food to an unknown woman at the Kyiv railway station. Then, with her son and an unliftable suitcase, she somehow made it to Romania, and there they kept making one mistake after another. They should've registered and received assistance, but Karina didn't do that. They should've stayed somewhere for free, but Karina and Yuri arranged to meet in Suceava, a city in Romania, and get a hotel room. So, they pay for things they could have gotten for free. They meet and hug each other. Yuri can't hold back his tears, while Karina, who throughout her travels has been dreaming of this moment—of how she'd finally melt into her husband's arms and weep—can't shed a tear.

And then they make more mistakes. They should've carefully picked their future country of relocation and their itinerary with the help of psychologists and volunteers in the humanitarian center. But Yuri and Karina run into some random acquaintances who are driving to Milan in their own car and can take them along. Yuri and Karina agree to go with them, but they have no idea why Italy is better for them than, let's say, Germany, or Belgium, or Spain. In Italy they can't find jobs or shelter, and in desperation they call their friend in Cologne. This friend is a doctor, and when Yuri and Karina call him, he's with patients—a middle-aged couple, Lutz and Galina. Their children have grown up and moved out, and now the couple lives by themselves in their spacious apartment. Yes, yes! They'd be happy to take the refugees into their home.

This seemed like a miracle, a happy coincidence; they got lucky. But while Yuri and Karina may have found their hosts by chance, Lutz and Galina became their hosts by design. They aren't overly religious, but there is a famous pastor in their town. This pastor used to help refugees during the Yugoslav Wars and the Syrian civil war. Now, because of this pastor, helping refugees has become a custom in their parish. This is what I mean by saying that, as a rule, people become hosts because they belong to a particular community.

The biggest communities are on the Internet, such as Facebook and Telegram. Alexander Auzan, dean of the School of Economics at Moscow State University, says that large social networks play a part in this war comparable to that of states. Great Britain protects the interests of British citizens, Germany takes care of German citizens, but Facebook—not as a commercial enterprise, but as a community of people—protects its own citizens, the members of Facebook.

When Rita Vinokur, one of the Rubikus community founders, is on call for the first time, and for the first time has to assign refugees to host families, the following message appears in her chatroom:

"Hello, we're a family of five, taking the train from Kraków to Berlin. We'll arrive in Berlin at midnight. What should we do?"

In Europe, it will be 8:00 P.M. In Pennsylvania, where Rita is, it's noon, thank God. There's some time left, but Rita is inexperienced and doesn't realize that someone will definitely volunteer to meet the refugee family and help them. She immediately starts searching for an apartment where she can accommodate five people, in literally four hours.

Rita has access to the Rubikus chatroom and has accounts on various social networks, and so she asks:

"Folks, who knows where I can find a place to stay for five people in Germany ASAP?" In response, she receives words of support—but they're not productive. Statements like "It's impossible to find an apartment for five people in four hours" are even less productive. But finally, she gets word that there's an apartment in Munich, and they're ready to take in the family. Hurrah! Rita begins searching for a driver with a car big enough for five people and their luggage and who'd be ready to meet the refugees at the train station at midnight and take them immediately across the country to Munich. There are more words of support in her chatroom—but they don't help. Some comment that such drivers don't exist, until finally she receives the following message—there's a driver with a minivan who's ready to take off from Berlin at midnight and take the refugee family anywhere, even to Mars.

Meanwhile Rita chats with this poor family and learns that none of them speaks any languages other than Russian and a little Ukrainian. This is bad because the driver speaks only German and a little English. They'll have to communicate using signs. Rita also learns that there's very little money left on the family's phone and they don't know how to add more money in Germany. And also ...

But then there's an unexpected blow. The host from Munich calls and apologizes, saying that he can't house any more people in his apartment. He's a very kind person but very absent-minded too. He lets anyone who asks stay in his apartment, but he totally forgot that a while ago he promised to host another family, and that family is moving in as we speak, all of them, with children, suitcases and a chinchilla.

And so, everything starts over. Once again, there's the Rubikus chatroom, social networks, useless comments about the impossibility of finding an apartment for five people in the two hours remaining, until finally someone in the chat mentions Woman-with-Swans. This woman lives in a faraway village. Several times she's contacted volunteer organizations on the Internet and offered her big house for refugees. Volunteers named her Women-with-Swans because her offers always come with bedroom pictures attached. Those bedrooms are in perfect German order: ironed comforters, neatly tucked-in blankets, and an Alpine-white towel folded in the shape of a swan on every bed.

So, everything is working out. The driver meets this family of five in Berlin. Woman-with-Swans waits for them until 5:00 A.M., then makes them a hot breakfast, treating them like family in her big house in the foothills of the Alps. And in Pennsylvania, Rita Vinokur is finishing her first shift with a feeling of deep satisfaction.

Here I'd like to point out one rather important fact. When our respectable Frau, who lives in a small Alpine village, decided to host refugees, she didn't post notices along her secluded mountain road, nor did she send her ad to a local newspaper or to a rentals site. She posted her ad on social networks. And the Ukrainian family of five, who didn't know any foreign languages, eventually figured out that they should ask the volunteer network Rubikus for help. And here is my conclusion—there must be a community where refugees and hosts can find one another. In other words, if you're present on social networks, you have a greater chance of finding a job and a place to live. If you don't use social media, but only watch TV, you'll be living in a hostel or a former shopping center, receiving limited welfare assistance and eating aid agency food while waiting for this endless war to be over so you can go back to your destroyed home.

OTHER PEOPLE'S CUSTOMS

In the first days after the refugees Karina and Yuri have settled into their new place, Galina cooks for them. She makes double the amount of food, as if her long-lost children had come back to live with them. It feels strange. But to cook and eat only vegetarian dishes feels even more strange—and you wouldn't cook two different dinners for the two families. In the beginning it was even interesting, but by the end of the first week, Galina is getting noticeably tired, while Karina still can't bring herself to help. Yuri is almost never home. Following those unwritten rules for refugees, he's rushing from one office to another, filling out papers, opening bank accounts, and trying to qualify for welfare assistance. It's all good, but he doesn't help with chores at home. And Karina and Yuri's son follows Galina like a lost puppy, asking her to go with him to the basement, where—as Galina herself had told him—the toys left by Galina's children are stored. Of course, it's very touching, but the boy distracts Galina from her work, and even more, Galina's no longer used to having a little boy around the house, a boy who seriously believes that the most important thing to do at this moment is to build a Lego tower.

Another issue is that Yuri and Karina are morning people, but Galina and Lutz are night owls. Galina makes dinner when Karina and Yuri can barely keep their eyes open, and their son is already asleep. And, for his part, the boy demands breakfast early in the morning, just a couple hours after Galina and Lutz have gone to bed.

It's good that the apartment is rather spacious, so that these two families with different habits can avoid bothering each other too much. It's also good that socially the families are similar: the Ukrainians work in the field of music and the Germans, in literature. It's good that Karina finally got used to their new situation and has taken over some of the household chores, at least for her family. It's good too that Yuri has qualified the family for welfare assistance and so has begun contributing to the budget. It's good that the families like each other and have somehow found some common ground in their everyday routines. Other families of hosts and refugees don't always manage to achieve that.

When Yuri and Karina are more settled, the pastor invites them to church with Galina and Lutz for a special service so the community will have a chance to meet them and collect charitable donations for their Ukrainian guests. In church, Yuri sings Italian arias and Ukrainian songs. The pastor gives a sermon. This is an unusual sermon, and the pastor delivers it with Yuri standing next to him. The pastor praises God for saving Karina and the little boy from bombing, for providing evacuation trains and buses to Romania, and for helping the Kovalchuk family reunite and find such wonderful hosts—Galina and Lutz. Yuri follows in his basic German and thanks god for having rescued his wife and son, for the evacuation trains, for reuniting the family, and for Galina and Lutz in Cologne. Meanwhile, Galina and Lutz sit in the fourth row and giggle. Over vegetarian dinners, Yuri had already tried to convert them to his religion, which is why they're giggling now.

"Amen!" the pastor says.

"Hare Krishna," Yuri repeats softly but with confidence. And here Lutz can't hold back his laughter any longer.

After the service, some parishioners stop to chat with Lutz. They barely know one another because Lutz doesn't believe in God and goes to church only on special occasions. These wealthy people live in big houses or apartments, and they want to ask Lutz how he managed to get himself refugees. They, too, would like to take refugees into their homes. They've written to government agencies, offering their hospitality, but have received no answers. Germany regularly pays money to refugees but can't organize its citizens to help those same refugees. These parishioners from Cologne have never heard about the Rubikus or any other volunteer organizations. All they had to do was fill in a request on the Rubikus site and they could've had a hundred refugees.

After the service, Galina doesn't go straight home—she needs to stop by the bank. There's a line inside. A refugee from Ukraine can't explain her problems to the clerk and can't understand the solutions the clerk is offering. The child with Down syndrome that the woman has brought with her interrupts her attempts to communicate with signs. Galina becomes a translator, and the refugee woman thanks her. Galina is mad at the state for giving money while not thinking about how the refugees will fill in the necessary documents without knowing the language. Neither Galina, nor the refugee woman, nor the clerk know anything about Rubikus. They could've filled in a request, and Rubikus would have found a volunteer to go with that woman to the bank and another to babysit the child. Rubikus would've made it easier for everyone.

Rubikus volunteers, however, receive plenty of complaints from both sides—from the refugees they followed from the firing line and from the hosts whose altruism they admire so much. Some complaints are serious, in which case they have to relocate the refugees, but others are comical, based on cultural misunderstandings.

One German host, for instance, seriously complains about the woman staying at his place: He believes she is systematically humiliating and physically abusing her seven-year-old son. The German doesn't understand her language but sees that every time the boy is getting ready for a walk, clumsily lacing his shoes while sitting on the floor, his mother yells at him, and as soon as the child reaches the door, she hits him on the head. The host tries to explain to his guest that such behavior is unacceptable, but she doesn't know German. He even called the police, but when the officer came and tried to talk to the woman, all she could do was shake her head and say *nicht verstehen*.

The woman claims to love her son dearly, pampering and coddling him. She fled Kharkiv, and for the twelve days they spent travelling to Germany, she was "fussing over the child like an eagle over an eaglet." And in regard to the screaming, the loving mother has never yelled at her darling son; it's the way she normally talks. And a smack on the back of the kid's head is purely symbolic—it helps to protect him from the evil eye. And as for the host, the woman is, of course, grateful, but in reality, he's a bore and a rat. So, the Rubikus volunteer has to explain, first to the German, the magic power of the Ukrainian smack on the back of the head and then to the Ukrainian woman that it's not customary in Europe to raise your voice or slap your child. Somehow the conflict is resolved.

But the next day brings a complaint from a Bavarian farmer. He hosted three refugee families and suggested they give him a hand and help a bit with the farm, so as not to be completely idle. Of course, if they had found a job, the farmer would never have asked them to take care of his potatoes and chickens, but all day long, they sit on the bench near the door and look at their phones. So, he tried to give them something to do, and what do you think? The women-refugees not only refused, but they also complained to the human rights feminist organizations, claiming they were being exploited and kept in slavery.

On another farm, the owner brought her guest some fresh milk from her cows for her child, but in response the refugee demanded lactose-free milk. Sorry, my cows don't produce lactose-free milk. The following day brings a complaint from a refugee who received his welfare assistance, and the host suggested that he contribute something to cover the cost of water and electricity—*How come, it's my money, isn't it?* And on the third day, there's a complaint from a refugee whose host asked how long he's planning to stay and if he's looking for a job and a place to live. *What an asshole, first he invites us and then tries to kick us out.*

When it comes to serious complaints, Spain holds first place. Many *albergues*, or hostels for pilgrims, that were transformed into refugee centers keep refugees locked up and feed them only rice and beans provided by the Red Cross. If someone wants to go to a city and look for a job, the staff threatens to not let them back in and to throw their belongings onto the street.

And of course, there were cases of fraud and sexual crime. I personally know of two cases when young women were invited to a comfortable house that turned out to be a brothel.

Nevertheless, it would be unfair to think that refugees have to deal with quarrels, scandals, and crimes all the time. I don't know how I'd behave if there were a family of total strangers living in my house. The overwhelming majority of refugees and hosts are of course decent people. But we must understand that when a human wave of several million rolls over the relatively small territory of Europe, scandals and crimes are bound to occur, if only in accordance with the law of large numbers.

Distributing Freedom

A total lack of trust toward the refugees is, however, the last thing we can afford. In the Romanian border town of Siret, right next to the checkpoint on the Ukrainian border, a young woman is standing and giving away cash to the refugees.

"Wait," she says, stopping an old woman or a mother with a kid. "Take some money."

"Me? I don't need it." This is typically the first reaction: People refuse to take the money.

"No-no, take it, please, you won't owe us anything. And you don't need to sign anything. We just want to help you. Please, take it and spend it any way you like. And go this way—there are volunteer tents with food, heat, and clothing."

Siret is a mountain town. In winter, it's very cold. The woman's name is Natasha Dukach. She's a violinist from Kharkiv, but for a long time she's been living in the US. Her husband, Semyon Dukach, who emigrated from the Soviet Union, is now a successful entrepreneur investing in ambitious IT projects. Their friend Alex Furman is also a Soviet émigré and successful businessman who owns genetic laboratories in California. His wife Marina . . . To make a long story short, these four founded the charitable organization Cash for Refugees. Actually, they didn't found the organization immediately; they began by traveling to the Ukrainian border to distribute their own money to refugees.

"Wait. Take this, please." "Me? No, I don't need it."

Alex tells me he arrived in Romania with twenty thousand dollars of his own money. But while he's been giving it away, about a hundred dollars per refugee in euros or Romanian leus, his friends have been transferring money into his account, totaling almost two hundred thousand additional dollars. And that's how it all started. It usually takes them more time to distribute the money than to receive charitable contributions. A week later, Alex returned to the States and registered their organization, which at that moment already had one and a half million dollars in its account. Then big sponsors joined in, along with Hollywood stars.

"What are we going to do when the IRS comes, and we'll have to file reports on all this money?" Alex kept asking Semyon.

"Well, they'll have to believe that we've given away all the money to refugees, or we'll have to pay taxes from our own money," Semyon answered. "We can afford it, can't we?"

When they could no longer give away the money all by themselves, they recruited volunteers. Every morning the volunteers would receive thick packets of money from Natasha, Alex, or Marina and spend the whole day distributing that money, trying to spot the old, the sick, and women with infants, and by evening they would bring back a report that no tax inspector would ever accept—a list with check marks; every check mark indicated a person who had received a modest cash donation.

At first, the Romanian police, fire fighters, soldiers, and the priest from the local church thought the Cash for Refugees volunteers were crooks, but they soon realized that they were just insane and so they began helping them—allowing them to stay right next to the border checkpoint and introducing them to the local authorities.

When the flow of refugees through Siret decreased and it became clear that most refugees wouldn't cross the border but would remain in Chernovtsy, housed in churches and gyms, the Cash for Refugee group moved to Chernovtsy. They set up an office, organized a data base, and began to give away money through the bank—by transferring around one hundred dollars onto the refugees' assistance cards. They calculated that to provide a one-time donation to two hundred thousand refugees would cost fifteen million dollars, and this was an achievable goal—they could raise that kind of money. Alex thought the Cash for Refugees would last a month or two, until big international organizations entered the scene. Now it seems that even the founders can't easily close their successful charity, which had been organized by chance. The donors were demanding that it continue. People like it when refugees receive not blankets or hot soup, but money.

"Because this way," Alex says, "we give them a bit of freedom. Yes, they are fed and dressed, but before February 24, they could not only have food and clothes—they could also decide if they should buy a cellphone charger or badminton rackets. They used to be as free as I am. Now, with this money, we're giving them back a little bit of freedom, and this is hard to stop. If there's famine in Africa, we'll go there too and distribute money—in other words, freedom, not just bread."

The Limits of Altruism

It's possible Alex is wrong. To tell the truth, it's impossible to be self-sacrificing for a long period of time. On the seventh day of her volunteer job at Medyka, Vika Lagodinskaya walks through the humanitarian center and runs into the very same woman who a day before couldn't let go of her daughter's hand, even for the time it took to go to the bathroom. Now the mother and daughter are walking next to each other; they're no longer holding hands. The woman recognizes Vika and hugs her. At this moment, Vika suddenly realizes she's dead tired and just can't deal with the refugees any longer. She can't translate their documents, listen to their tragic stories, or even be happy about their good news. Thank God, tomorrow her shift will be over. How right were the Israeli psychologists when they decided to invite volunteers for no more than a week—in a week's time, a volunteer burns out.

Evgeny Pinelis has been working in Przemyśl for ten days. He's completely happy, feels like he's in the right place, and—a true indicator of psychological balance—doesn't even browse through the news or listen every night to the Ukrainian president's adviser Oleksiy Arestovych. But on the tenth day Evgeny feels as if a light bulb has been turned off inside of him. The vacation he decided to use volunteering is almost over, and Evgeny is glad to go back home to New York to work as a critical care doctor—apparently, it's much easier than working as a paramedic in a refugee camp.

Olga Sokolova is sleeping. She's been sleeping for twenty-three hours straight, almost an entire day. In Moscow, Olga runs a successful wine business. She's a smart, modern, and fashionable woman who loves traveling. But now she feels ashamed to travel through Europe when in the East her countrymen are traveling in tanks or on evacuation trains.

Olga says she's like a cat: She needs freedom of movement. She says, "I might not go anywhere, but the door must be open." Since the COVID pandemic, Olga has packed an "emergency travel bag," containing a bank card issued in Malta (which became very handy after February 24), two foreign passports, some cash in dollars and euros, three Pfizer vaccination certificates—these days, that's what sets a person free.

Since the beginning of the war, Olga feels strange when she watches the news: historic events are occurring, but she isn't a part of them. But she should be. She must witness with her own eyes the people whose cities and lives we've destroyed. She needs to know how much they hate us now. With these thoughts weighing on her, Olga is searching for airplane tickets to Berlin to work for a week or so at the Central railway station as a volunteer and translator for refugees. That's how successful businesspeople spend their vacations these days.

There are no direct flights from Russia to Berlin anymore. To fly through Istanbul costs a thousand euros, through Abu Dhabi—three thousand, so Olga flies to Minsk, takes a bus to Vilnius, and from Vilnius flies to Berlin. Friends meet her in every city. As I've been saying, in order to live a more or less normal life under conditions of war and be in a position to help others, you, too, must constantly receive help from people with whom you are virtual friends on social networks.

At the Berlin Central Station, Olga goes through an orientation and learns what opportunities exist for refugees and where to find them; she then receives a volunteer uniform vest with a yellow chevron—indicating that she knows Russian. In addition, she attaches a sticker on her vest informing everyone that the person with this sticker knows both Russian and English.

Outfitted in this way, Olga walks back and forth through the station. From time to time, other volunteers ask her to translate something for them. Occasionally, she sees a group of teenagers, approaches them (as per her instructions), inquires about their parents, and then asks them to call their mothers to make sure they're not lost or runaways. Olga chats for a while with these teenagers, and they talk about the war. The thing that scares these teens the most is that President Zelenskyy might stop the war before total victory and make peace in exchange for territory. "No," the teenagers say, "we need to bring this war to an end, free all Ukrainian land, including the Donbas and Crimea." But, despite all that, they don't hate Russians. Olga is Russian, and she doesn't hide the fact that she's from Moscow. "So what?" the teenagers say. "We hate only those who attacked us."

It sometimes happens that, after a train has arrived and the crowd of passengers has subsided, a couple of elderly unattended people are left sitting on their suitcases on the platform.

"Hello, are you refugees?" Olga approaches them.

"Yes."

"But why are you sitting here?"

"We don't know where to go."

Olga grabs their suitcases and drags them to the escalator, gets them tickets to Dusseldorf, which, as it happens, was their destination; it's where their daughter lives. Then she explains to the old couple that it's better to take the direct train in the morning than to travel now with two layovers—you'll arrive faster on a direct train. Then she arranges their overnight stay.

"Here in Germany, you Russians are so kind," the old couple says. "Why are you so angry in Moscow?"

"I'm a Russian from Moscow," Olga states, not hiding the fact.

"Why did you do this to us?" the old woman says through her tears, and the women hug each other.

Olga has endured such volunteer walks through the railway station for three days. After that she moves out of her friend's place where she's been staying in Berlin, gets a hotel room, and goes to bed. She sleeps for almost an entire day. The human capacity for active altruism and empathy is limited.

Chapter 5
Rubikus and Others

> "The elimination of over one hundred nationalists and mercenaries from Western countries as the result of a high precision air strike by Iskander operational-tactical rockets on the defense headquarters of the City of Kharkhov has been confirmed. Russia continues to fulfill the humanitarian responsibilities it has assumed to save and protect civilians. Despite all the difficulties and obstacles created by Kiev over the past several days, without the participation of either the Ukrainian authorities or the UN High Commissioner for Refugees and the International Committee of the Red Cross, 14168 individuals, including 891 children, have been evacuated from danger zones in Ukraine to Russia." Official Telegram Channel of the Russian Ministry of Defense, March 25, 2022.

The Chatroom

"I have a request from two elderly people in Chernigov. They don't want to go by boat. Are there any other options?" Since February 25, 2022, Svetlana Vodolazskaya has begun every day with this or some similar message. She wakes up, checks her chatroom, and sees . . . "No, there's nothing else available in Chernigov, only a boat."

It was by mere chance that Svetlana started her volunteer group within the Rubikus community—which the organizers and participants of the Hamelin music festival had been using to stay in touch. She saw a request to help some refugees—to find an evacuation train, figure out where to go, arrange for someone to meet them . . . First, she began by giving advice, then got more deeply involved, and brought in her friends.

"Free flights to the UK—are you sure it's not a scam? Do they need to pay for their luggage?"

"To begin with, why are they going to the UK? Look, it's written in every booklet that it's very hard to live in the UK without money."

Actually, Svetlana is a tutor—she helps children with math. When Russia annexed Crimea, Svetlana and her husband left the country. Her husband is a computer programmer and easily found a job in London. Even before moving to London, Svetlana used to teach online, but now her school is truly international—children from all over the world sign up for her classes. And on top of that, she organizes a summer math camp in Austria, as well as a festival in Hamelin, Germany, which offers music lessons, classes on various academic subjects, workshops on various crafts, and conversation and reading practice in Russian.

"Listen, what do we have in Bulgaria? My request is at a hotel right on the Golden Sands Beach, but they feed them very poorly. According to the mother, her kid is literally starving. For lunch they got two chicken wings, and for dinner some bean salad. She's asking for a slow cooker, to feed her child."
"I found a store in Varna where they'll sell a slow cooker at a discount. And here's what they write from Varna: It's true, the food is bad. The state subsidy is only twenty euros a day, and many hotels haven't received any money yet."

There are thirty-five teachers working at the online school Svetlana organized. They formed the initial backbone of Rubikus. Very soon, more people joined, mostly parents who had taken their kids to the Hamelin festival or to the math camp in Austria. In a few days, seventy-eighty people had joined from the States, the UK, Germany, Poland, and Russia. Thanks to the geographic distribution of the volunteers in different time zones, Rubikus is able to work non-stop, without any breaks for sleep.

"Welcome, Diana. This chat was created for those who are willing to help our team with the evacuation of refugees from

Ukraine to Europe. To receive access to our database, please fill out this form . . . "

Svetlana often conducts interviews with new Rubikus volunteers. She usually asks where the volunteer is physically located, how much time they can devote, how much stress they can withstand, and so on. Svetlana used to think that volunteer efforts to evacuate refugees would be necessary only in the first days, maybe the first weeks, of the war. Then the "grownups" would step in—the Red Cross, the UN High Commissioner for Refugees, and government agencies in the countries bordering Ukraine would arrive and rescue everyone. But "the grownups" haven't showed up or they arrived many months later, and when they finally arrived, they asked Rubikus for help. Meanwhile, the Rubikus network continues to grow, and the work of its volunteers is still in high demand.

"Is it true that in Switzerland, it costs 850 franks to call an ambulance? Why is everything so expensive there? Or is there a way to get it for free for the refugees?"

"My request received visas for adults, but not for the children. She just forgot to apply for kids' visas. Now they're sitting and waiting."

In the slang of the Rubikus volunteers, a request refers to a person or a family.

"In Przemyśl, a very good guy's done everything from Dnipro—he met my request and put them on the bus."

Translated from the volunteer slang into normal language, this statement from the chat means that there's a new Rubikus volunteer in Przemyśl who's been effective in organizing transportation for a refugee or a refugee family from the city of Dnipro to the Polish border. The volunteer met the family and sent them to their final destination. Incidentally, the word "request" can also be used literally, as in a request for help.

"There are volunteers in Warsaw who can help with tickets within Europe. They used to send people to Canada and

Mexico too, but not anymore. For that, you have to come in person, file a request, then wait for a couple of days. Some Polish fund finances this."

At the beginning of the war, Rubikus dealt mostly with streams of refugees coming from Poland and Romania. By May, most people were arriving through Narva and Tallinn, coming from the Russian side. They were refugees from Mariupol, Rubizhne, Popasna, and Kharkiv—those who had wanted to evacuate to the West but were forced to evacuate to the East.

Very soon there were volunteers in Russia who were prepared to collect money and buy tickets to Europe for people in the Russian refugee centers. And again, no "grownups" stepped forward to cover those expenses—not the Red Cross, nor the UNHCR—only volunteers.

As far as Svetlana knows, no one from the "grownups"—the Ministry of Education or the Children Rights Commissioners—have given any thought to how refugee children will study without knowing the language of the country that accepted them.

"Two of my families got accepted into Finland. Of course, it's crazy cold over there LOL, and there's the language that no one understands, but they welcomed them as family. And right away they went to live with their host families."

Svetlana proposes that the next big initiative for Rubikus is to organize schools where refugee children can study. In addition, Svetlana is planning to finish designing the Rubikus website so that it can gather in one place information about all the stipends and social programs offered to refugees by universities from around the world. Svetlana believes that young adults are in an especially difficult situation. Little children will learn the language and assimilate, but teenagers without the language won't be able to continue their education, not this year or the next. So, Svetlana's school is primarily for them. During the first months of the war, Svetlana realized that "the grownups" weren't going to show up, weren't going to rescue anybody, and weren't going to fix anything. We're "the grownups" now.

Organizing the Process

"I'm ready to do GoForma for Pampers in Bulgaria."
"What are you ready to do?"
"LOL! Gofundme, not GoForma. Sorry."

To be honest, in the beginning the messages in the Rubikus chatroom, where I was added in the first days of the war, looked like a barely comprehensible hodgepodge of information. And even if someone shared some useful information with their colleagues, it was impossible to find it the next day under the avalanche of new cases, questions, and random volunteer conversations.

"I have a request. A battery and power supply specialist is looking for a job. What country is best for him?"

"There's a refugee support program in Andorra. They're offering a job in the alternative energy field, the salary is 1100 euro a month, free travel to Spain, free housing until the first paycheck, medical insurance, and kindergartens, schools, and language courses for the children."

All these messages were landing in the same chatroom until Rita Vinokur joined Rubikus and decided to organize things.

Rita is a native Muscovite but has been living in Minsk since getting married. Her husband, of course, is a computer programmer (no, not all Rubikus volunteers are computer programmers; there are also musicians, educators, wives of computer programmers, and owners of small IT companies). After the 2020 Minsk protests, they decided to leave Belarus. As Rita puts it, "We wanted to live in accordance with our conscience and to live in safety at the same time." They easily found jobs in Pennsylvania and moved to a small town where squirrels run across the roofs, and the main reason for driving slowly is to avoid hitting a deer crossing the road. But as soon as they settled down, the war started. The first week, Rita was beside herself with shock and worry. (How well I understand her—I, too, was going nuts until I began collecting the material for this book.) But in week two, on social media, she found the volunteer group Rubikus and offered Svetlana Vodolazskaya her help.

The first thing Rita set about doing was to build a database. Now, for example, the announcement that the city Andorra in the Spanish province of Teruel is offering refugees jobs in the alternative energy field won't get lost in the endless flow of volunteer chats, but will be carefully placed in a designated cell of a Google table, and this information can easily be retrieved by searching under "job," "energy," or "Andorra." In addition to information about jobs, guidelines for filling out paperwork, and rules for crossing borders, the database contains extensive, constantly expanding lists of hosts, drivers, and refugees—those who are now traveling with logistical support from Rubikus and those whom Rubikus evacuated from Ukraine and helped relocate in Europe. In April of 2022, there were two thousand families settled in Europe.

Every Thursday, Rita leads an orientation for new volunteers. For forty minutes, she teaches them how to use the database, which has already become quite large and complicated. Another forty minutes are devoted to dealing with refugee requests. This orientation is mandatory, and without it you may sympathize with the refugees and even participate in the group chats, but you can't receive a request from a real person and try to help them leave Ukraine.

"Today (April 28) at 8:00 P.M. Ukrainian time, there will be an orientation. Everyone is welcome."

"I've been already but wouldn't mind listening again. Don't think I got everything. Can I?"

"EVERYONE is welcome."

The main thing Rita teaches is not to promise the refugees the impossible. Let me summarize the forty-minute lecture in a few words. First, a volunteer should introduce themselves, so the person who sent their request to Rubikus knows they're talking with a real person who feels bad for them and is ready to help. Second, a volunteer should not present all options (Rubikus is not a travel agency) but should ask where the person wants to go and why they have chosen that place. If a refugee doesn't know where they want to go, the volunteer should ask leading questions regarding their age, occupation, number of family members, and whether they have any pets. These questions should significantly narrow the range of options. If a refugee insists on going to Warsaw or Berlin, but the volunteer knows these cities are overcrowded, then the volunteer should honestly explain this to the refugee and say, "I'll search for opportunities for you in Berlin, but the chances are low, so maybe we should check options in other cities, just in case."

If a refugee is not a person with a disability, elderly, a pregnant woman, or the mother of a large family who hopes to travel to the site of their relocation in a comfortable car with a selfless driver, then the volunteer should explain to this refugee that there are buses and trains. A volunteer is prepared to find them a convenient itinerary and to send them schedules, but drivers of private cars are reserved for those who truly cannot use public transportation. Even though there is a long list of such drivers, they can only help refugees in their free time, and there are never enough available drivers for people in need.

Once a refugee reaches their destination, the volunteer should explain to them politely and compassionately, but also decisively, that their request is now closed and that Rubikus is not responsible for any future problems related to this request. Rubikus is a group that organizes refugee evacuation and resettlement; it does not provide life-long consultations. Of course, if something doesn't go the way it should, a refugee may, for old times' sake, call their volunteer and ask for advice. And, of course, a volunteer may once again offer help by providing the refugee with booklets on how stores work, let's say, in Germany or Italy (many people are used to the stores working 24-7) or governmental offices (many people think they need to bribe the officials), but it's not wise to overextend such help. It's better to give the refugee information about local volunteer organizations, wish them luck, and say goodbye. Because the stream of new refugees shows no signs of stopping.

For refugees, word of mouth works better than Google. From the first days of her work at Rubikus, Rita noticed that it was very hard to Google the schedules of evacuation trains and buses or the addresses of human rights, women rights, and other organizations that help refugees. Rita tested this by entering specific searches—"evacuation from Ukraine," "help for refugees," and "Rubikus"—and the results were almost zero. She was getting links for the Hamelin festival, the Austrian math camp, but not for one of the most active organizations providing aid to refugees. Rita even asked her husband, the computer-programmer, why this was happening, but he only shrugged his shoulders—Who knows? Could it mean that Google is designed for a society of consumers and so doesn't work that well for a society where people help people?

"THE CITY" OF REFUGEES

By the way, not everyone is able to follow this sensible rule: help the refugees escape and get settled, and after that—leave them alone. Many volunteers continue helping their requests. For Alya Khaitlina, for instance, this became her main job. Alya is a poet. From the first day of the war, she's kept a poetic diary on Telegram where she writes about Rubikus's work:

It's as if paintings drift before my eyes—
A blossoming tree. Then there are tanks in the frame.
Even in our dreams, we continue to search for apartments,
Load trucks, request humanitarian aid.
Work, meet, explain, cry, and get frustrated,
Call total strangers and feel totally different ourselves.
Do anything so as not to see the news, that is, the faces,
The remains, to be precise—a date, a place, a name.

In some way, Alya's poems are like the Rubikus chatrooms—not entirely understandable to outsiders, to those who haven't gone through Rita Vinokur's orientation sessions and don't have any experience with the evacuation of refugees. But for those inside the group, this is all extremely recognizable, just as you always recognize your native language in any corner of the world. This is what drives them—the impossibility of looking the refugees in the eye. So, they busy themselves with paperwork and logistics, occupying their hands and minds, day and night, so as not to look into their eyes.

But Alya is a linguist too. Her unfinished dissertation is about bilingual families, about the children who first master their mother's language and their father's, and so are able, better than anyone else, to help their parents understand and be understood in their new country. This is their main hope: Their children will assimilate and help them to assimilate too.

Now Alya can see her dissertation coming to life before her eyes, in Munich, on the Arnulfstraße, in the center named "The City," where Alya works. It's not easy to describe this center. It's a school and a club for bilingual families living in Munich. On February 24, Alya went to an anti-war demonstration, where in the crowd of protesters she made a number of new friends, and these German students and young people became members of the center. They loaded humanitarian aid, tents, foam mats, sleeping bags, food, and water, then designed a city guide for the refugees, translated documents, and helped find accommodations. Every day ten-fifteen families passed through the center. In the first month of the war, a total of fifteen thousand refugees came to Bavaria, six thousand of them to Munich. By April, there were no available apartments in Munich, and the work of the center switched to assimilating the refugees that had already arrived and settled there.

The center rented an additional floor in their building on Arnulfstraße and organized an info-hub: They set up four tables, put a volunteer behind each table, and from morning to night, they answered all kinds of questions from the refugees. They successfully demanded that every government office assign an *Ansprechpartner*, an official who is prepared to answer any questions the center's volunteers might have about their department and who is on call during working hours. Then they organized an art-hub—offering lessons in music, painting, and other arts that help the refugees communicate, assimilate, and channel their emotions. Next, they organized a playground for the kids, a place where the parents can now leave them for a few hours—which is a great help in Bavaria, where daycare is a problem. Without daycare, parents won't be able to find a job and will have to continue living on welfare.

The City's school expanded to 230 students, and to accommodate them, Ukrainian teachers were hired—a win-win solution: The children could study, and the adults could work. And those teachers who didn't find a job at The City were referred by the center to the public schools where, starting in September, there would be welcome classes—remedial classes designed to help the children learn German and adapt to the unknown environment.

And, finally, they organized a Ukrainian festival—a real celebration with Ukrainian music, Ukrainian food, fundraising (of the give-what-you-can variety), and the perplexed faces of the celebrants.

The collected donations were for medications. Medications for special cases.

The Special Cases

"I have here two elderly women with nineteen cats and two dogs. They don't want to leave their animals behind under the bombing. What should I do?"

Alex Guryevich from Israel4Ukraine refers to such cases as special, and Svetlana Vodolazskaya from Rubikus calls them tasks with an asterisk. It seems only logical not to waste any time on two crazy cat-lovers who are willing to risk their lives for their cats, but Anna Tsimelzon and other volunteers from Rubikus see these cases as personal challenges. Within two months a volunteer dealing with the evacuation of refugees can become a highly skilled professional and, as is customary with professionals, they welcome difficult cases and the opportunity to brag to their colleagues. It's like in city parks before the war, when boys used to show off in front of girls and one another by demonstrating their skills on bicycles or skateboards. To evacuate two women with nineteen cats and two dogs? You call *this* an impossible case? Just watch me! Where are they? The Kharkiv region? We'll look for a nearby shelter for abandoned animals and request ten cat carriers (two cats per bag) and two dog crates. Then we'll look for a minibus, load the cat ladies and their charges into the bus, drive them across the border, find a place that's willing to host two women with two cats, and take the remaining pets to a nearby shelter where the ladies can visit them. Bingo!

They're ready to begin the rescue operation, when a better option arises—a farm in Northern Poland where the owners are willing to take refugees with animals, even livestock, and the two women are welcome to stay there with all their cats and dogs.

"A woman with cerebral palsy, 45 years old, a Ph.D. She's trapped in a basement. She can no longer walk or take care of herself."

An impossible case? Difficult, but not impossible. Svetlana Vodolazskaya finds a car to take the woman to the Polish border. From there, another car takes her to the ferry to Latvia. In Latvia, she is admitted to a rehabilitation center for adults with cerebral palsy. How many rehabilitation centers did you have to call?! Not that many. Svetlana says it's important to have a general idea about where to settle a particular refugee. In this case, to know from the start that you're looking for an adult rehabilitation center and not call people around the world screaming "Help!" Then every fourth call will usually be successful.

But there are failures too.

"D., a second BMT in Turkey. The government promised to pay for it but couldn't because of the war."

This record from the chatroom in the bird-like language of the Rubikus volunteers has to be deciphered. Once upon a time, there was a girl who, if I'm not mistaken, was twelve years old. The girl's name was D. She was diagnosed with leukemia. To treat the leukemia, D. needed a bone marrow transplant. Before the war, the Ukrainian government paid for D.'s bone marrow transplant surgery in Turkey. The surgery took place, but D.'s body rejected the bone marrow cells, as sometimes happens. The second transplant operation was scheduled in the same Turkish hospital, and again the Ukrainian government was going to pay for it. But then the war began.

Theoretically, it was possible to transport D. to Germany, where her refugee status would provide her with medical insurance, and then she could have the second bone marrow transplant in any clinic in Germany and the German taxpayers would pay for it. So, why didn't they do that? Why did they decide to take the girl back to Turkey? Was it because oncologists frown on transferring a patient from one clinic to another in the middle of treatment without special circumstances? But in this case, there were special circumstances to justify changing not just the hospital but the country too. Especially since, as you may recall, in Turkey medical insurance for refugees doesn't cover cancer . . .

In other words, not only did the Rubikus volunteers organize D.'s evacuation from Ukraine to Turkey, but they were also raising money to pay for the girl's surgery. They needed to raise a rather large sum, almost three hundred thousand euros, but managed to raise only eight thousand. The girl's parents raised some money too, the clinic made some adjustments, and the second operation was performed. But it didn't save the girl. Would she have survived if Rubikus had sent her to Germany? No one can say.

Alex Guryevich from Israel4Ukraine was faced with a similar case. A fifteen-year-old girl with a serious pathology of the spinal cord—she couldn't walk; she could only sit in a wheelchair. And she'd been sitting in a wheelchair in a basement in Sumy for two weeks under Russian attacks.

To rescue her, Alex called—can you guess?—the Health Ministry of Israel. And they provided him with an ambulance, and not your typical ambulance but an armored one. (Israel sent a few of those to transport refugees from Ukraine). So, the girl was driven to Lviv in an armored ambulance.

It's March, the weather outside is cold, and night is falling. Life in Lviv is almost normal; even some cafés are open. It suddenly becomes clear to Alex that he's made a mistake. He arranged for the girl to spend a couple of nights with a host family, so she wouldn't have to sleep on the floor in the refugee camp. But the hosts forgot to mention that they live on the third floor of a building without an elevator—an impossible situation for a girl in a wheelchair. What's the next step? Zoom, WhatsApp, Telegram, and Viber. That night Alex set a record—in Lviv, a city overloaded with refugees, in forty minutes he managed to find an apartment on the first floor. The girl barely felt the cold.

Alex managed to set yet another record, not in terms of time but in terms of quantity, when he evacuated an entire nursing home—fifty-two elderly people—from Dnipro. It was a Jewish nursing home, but there were some Ukrainians and Russians living there too. Originally, this nursing home was created by the famous Dnipro synagogue as a place for elderly Jews, but those elderly Jews would talk about their friends and neighbors, also lonely, with whom they sat together on the benches in their apartment courtyards and complain about their hard life. Gradually, the nursing home began taking in non-Jewish people as well. There were more than fifty residents when the war began.

The request from the nursing home came from two old women—they filled in the Israel4Ukraine paperwork and communicated with Alex. One of those women was paralyzed, and the other was blind. One could write, and the other could talk on the phone. The other nursing home inhabitants were even more frail. Most of the nurses and orderlies had left; only two or three of the most unselfish stayed. These orderlies managed to keep the old people clean, but they had no time to cook, and, anyway, the food supplies were almost gone. And those sweet old ladies didn't understand how to communicate with a smartphone with some stranger from Israel. So, he could probably help the Jews, but what to do with the non-Jewish residents?

In any case, the Jewish community brought food and water to the nursing home the next day—Alex had been able to reach them by phone, convincing them to help. Several volunteers began feeding the old people. They fed everybody. I mean, who could possibly feed only the Jews in front of hungry Ukrainians on the adjoining beds.

Meanwhile, Alex was calling the assistant of the Jewish billionaire, against whom a criminal case had been filed in Ukraine, asking him to pay for the buses to evacuate the entire nursing home. The billionaire agreed to pay.

Then Alex found a hospice in Poland and brought the old people there.

While telling me this story, Alex repeats an obvious fallacy. He says that there are no nationalities in the world. I argue, "How can you say that? Just look around. The Russians hate the Ukrainians, and the Ukrainians hate the Russians. And during the last war, Germans, Jews, Poles, Ukrainians, and Russians—everyone hated one another, they all hated one another.

But Alex insists: There are no nationalities, no citizenships, no allegiances. There is only humanity, and the lack of thereof—nothing else is real.

When he repeats this for the third time and the fourth time, it finally dawns on me—he's talking about the future. About a world that's being born in the flames of this war. About a world that has yet to be built. About a world that must become our new reality when the war is over.

Chapter 6
To the East

"Under conditions of extreme opposition by Ukrainian authorities, since the start of the special military operation, 419736 individuals, including 88373 children, have been evacuated from danger zones in Ukraine and the Lugansk and Donetsk People's Republics to Russia. 49362 personal vehicles have crossed the border into the Russian Federation." Official Telegram Channel of the Russian Ministry of Defense, March 25, 2022.

A Roma Song

It's clear at a glance that Irina Grinyova is a very good person, kind and sympathetic. Before February 24, she'd worked as the director of Seven Steps, a rehabilitation center for people with disabilities in Voronezh. In this isolated building located on the outskirts of the city, people with disabilities would get medical help, learn a trade that would allow them to earn a living and live independently, take driving lessons, and occasionally organize social events.

As soon as the war began, the residents were kicked out, and Seven Steps was transformed into a temporary accommodation center for refugees. And Irina Grinyova automatically became the director of this center, too. Some changes had to be made. Beds were set up in the offices and corridors, additional tables were added in the dining hall, and Putin's portrait now appeared in Grinyova's office. It seems that there was no Putin in the office before—I mean, why would you need the President's portrait in a center for people with disabilities? But refugees are a political matter and, following either an official memo or her own managerial instinct, Grinyova acquired the portrait, but it never made it onto the wall behind the director's desk; instead, it was placed modestly on a small file cabinet.

Refugees from the occupied territories of Ukraine, those who were unable or unwilling to cross the frontline and evacuate to the West, travelled here or to Voronezh, Belgorod, Rostov, and Bryansk regions—and now, to the rest of Russia. Some drive their own cars, damaged and dented by shrapnel. Grinyova hides these cars in the back because the owners are afraid the locals will see the Ukrainian license plates, decide they belong to the enemy, and destroy the cars completely. Or some mysterious partisans will sneak in from Ukraine, decide the owners of these cars are traitors, and destroy them. In short, Grinyova hides these cars and tries to reach a deal with the local auto shop owners to repair them at a discounted rate.

All day long Grinyova walks down the corridors of her three-floor Center and checks on everything—whether the refugees are comfortably settled in, whether they're getting enough food, whether they've received clothing and personal hygiene items supplied by the aid agencies. She does so much walking that she's changed her usual high-heel pumps for sneakers; otherwise her legs would be worn out by the end of the day.

And the refugees lie on their beds. Ninety-seven people—thirty-eight men (the martial law preventing men from leaving Ukraine doesn't apply in the occupied territories), thirty-four women, twenty-five children, including seven preschoolers and two people with disabilities—all of them are lying on their beds and breaking the most important rule for refugees: Don't lie down during the day.

The Center's staff tries to involve the children in some activities, drawing and games, but the children aren't interested—they prefer to lie on their beds and look at their phones. Grinyova invites specialists from the local banks and employment services to the Center so they can help the refugees open bank accounts, register for unemployment benefits, and find jobs. But in most cases those attempts are hindered by a lack of documents, and after the specialists leave, the refugees lie back down.

Sometimes journalists and reporters from the leading Russian TV networks visit. They have an authoritative air and behave like officers inspecting an army regiment. Grinyova tells the journalists that the refugees are tired, shocked by the war, and don't want to give any interviews, but the reporters inform her in a commanding voice that they have direct orders from the powers that be to interview the refugees—and they *will* interview them. Alyona Klyuchka, who used to work as a former clerk at the City Hall of Tsyrkuny, a small town near Kharkiv, avoids their questions. Zakhary B., a driver who found a way to buy bread from his colleagues without standing in line, thanks them and tells them how the Ukrainian authorities limited his freedom, how he welcomes the war and calls it a war of liberation. After that, both return to their rooms (each family has their own room) and lie down.

Alyona wants to go to the West but doesn't know how. She even has some money (some real savings actually), but it's in Ukranian hryvnias or on her Visa card. No one will exchange hryvnias in Russia, and Visa cards issued outside of Russia are not accepted anywhere. A one-time payment of ten thousand rubles promised by the Russian government (compare this to a monthly payment of 500 euros refugees receive in Germany) has yet to be paid and will be awarded only when a refugee has registered and opened a bank account. Alyona doesn't know anything about volunteer organizations that help with emigration.

Zakhary wants to stay in Russia, find a job, and rent an apartment—he's full of hope. But there are no jobs, no registration, no payments—all this takes time. They have clothes and a roof over their heads, but no opportunities. There's only one thing left to do—lie down. The entire system of Russian temporary accommodations for refugees is designed to compel people to lie passively on their backs all day long. Grinyova, whose previous job was to teach people with disabilities how to become active and independent, proposes that her new charges at least go for a walk to the nearby forest—it's so nice over there, fresh spring air, untouched nature, but the refugees say they're afraid to leave the Center and continue lying on their beds.

The elderly couple Lyubov Alexandrovna and Nikolay Petrovich, who's great-granddaughter's birthday was the day the war began, lie quietly in the hallway. And their grandchildren and great-granddaughter lie in a room close by. But they too don't really talk; they just look at their cellphones.

The Roma Ira lives with her youngest son, who is almost sixteen years old. Her older son is about twenty; he lives in the next room with his very young wife and their eight-month-old son. They've come to visit Ira, and everyone finds a place to sit on the two beds—the only other furniture that can fit in the room is a nightstand.

You don't need to ask Ira about anything—she volunteers her story, which sounds like a mournful Roma song or lament.

"We used to live with my youngest son in Khartsyzk, and my oldest son lived in Kharkiv. When a missile hit the house, we fled. We hitchhiked all the way to my oldest son's, and he put us all in the car, and off we went. We only got as far as Volchansk, where the bridge had been destroyed. So, we got out of the car and crossed the river by stepping on logs, and then we walked for five hours through empty fields until we reached Shebekino. My daughter-in-law is so young, it was hard for her to carry the baby, so we all took turns carrying the baby. And only at the border did we realize that we'd left our documents at home. They let my oldest son with his young wife and baby go through, and they fed the baby. But my younger son and I had to wait for three hours, because we were without documents."

When Ira talks, she sways as if she's singing:

"At my age, I should just go back home. But how can I go back? Maybe we'll go further. My sons are in construction, my daughter-in-law works too, she's a cook. And I could sell nuts, it's a traditional Roma trade to sell nuts. They offered my sons jobs at a construction site. But for those jobs, they'd have to turn in their passports for an entire year. How can you turn in your passport? I know how it is to live without a passport—there's no life without a passport. Without a passport, I can't get any assistance or open a bank account."

(Irina Grinyova, by the way, denies such accusations—she's absolutely sure that none of the recruiters at the Center would ever demand passports as collateral. Grinyova says that most likely they were asked to turn in their passports for a couple of days to register and obtain a migration card.)

But Ira continues her lament:

"We have relatives in Russia. They live near Krasnodar, they live near Stavropol, but we can't get there. My brother lives there, but we can't reach him. We aren't in our country, to tell you the truth. If they gave us an allowance, we would've bought a ticket and would've gone to my brother's, or to another brother's—all Romas are brothers. We could've worked and sold nuts, we could've bought a house. Even if it were only a shack, it would've been ours. But they don't let us.

"And so I went to Sberbank. They talked to me. They knew they wouldn't give me a card without my original passport, but they talked to me anyway. Because we're Romas, you can talk to us and not give us anything. They talked to us nicely, they treated us well, but they didn't give us anything. We, Romas, only want what's ours, but we've lost it all. And now our baby is afraid of the wind and sun."

A Children's Camp

At night, when the children are already in bed, Nadezhda Ivanovna listens to the howling of a dog. It's her dog. Nadezhda

Ivanovna listens to her dog howling over the phone. She calls her former neighbor, and if there's no shelling, the neighbor takes her phone and some dog food, goes to Nadezhda Ivanovna's house, and lets her listens:

"U-u-u-u-u-u!"

"Eat, my sweetie, eat."

"U-u-u-u-u-u!"

"Eat, damn it! Why are you howling as if someone died?"

Nadezhda Ivanovna tries to talk to her dog through the phone, but the dog doesn't understand phones.

Over there, in the city of Stakhanov (Ukrainians call it Kadiivka), Nadezhda Ivanovna used to be the director of an orphanage. Before 2014, she worked for the Ukrainian Department of Education. After 2014, when, with the support of Russia, the Luhansk and Donetsk regions declared their independence and the military confrontation began, the orphanage fell under the jurisdiction of the so-called Luhansk People's Republic. But no one harmed the orphans—neither the Ukrainian authorities, nor the separatists. Over the entire eight years of the war in Eastern Ukraine, from 2014 to 2022, no one bombed or shelled Stakhanov. The residents would hear occasional explosions and shots, but, as Nadezhda Ivanovna recounts, that was far from Kadiivka, on the demarcation line. There was practically no war, or it was a small and distant war.

On February 18, 2022, one week before the big war started, the Russian army entered Kadiivka, and Nadezhda Ivanovna was allocated two buses and ordered by the Department of Education to evacuate the children to Russia. Of the staff, only women should accompany the orphans. All the men—one guard and a handyman—had to stay behind.

The children treated the trip more like an entertaining field trip. They watched the Russian soldiers in the street with the same interest children in Moscow watch preparations for a parade. They boarded the buses and off they went. When they reached Rostov, they boarded a train. Then, when they reached Voronezh, they again boarded busses, which took them to the summer resort Lipki, which was owned by the Russian Railway Company.

The keyword here is "summer," but it was February. All the buildings were practically unlivable. The walls were built for summer, with a single layer of bricks, all the windows had gaps, the doors were not insulated, and neither was the plumbing, which got frozen and clogged up as soon as they tried to use it. Nadezhda Ivanovna—who resembles a sphere, a bundle of energy emitting ungrounded optimism—was running through the building passing out blankets to the children and checking to make sure that every child was wearing two sweaters. There weren't enough sweaters, and so Nadezhda Ivanovna called social services in Voronezh, children rights organizations, and the Committee on the Rights of the Child. She demanded help, and finally help began to arrive.

First, a local beekeeper arrived with a whole barrel full of honey. To make sure the children didn't overindulge, he placed the barrel in Nadezhda Ivanovna's office. The barrel is too heavy to move, and so she distributes the honey from her room. Every evening at dessert time, a line forms and Nadezhda Ivanovna gives every child some honey with a ladle.

Then—Hallelujah!—company representatives (Nadezhda Ivanovna doesn't remember the name of the company) arrived and brought powerful heaters. They installed the heaters in the hallways and near the doors; the building gradually grew warmer, and in three days the bedrooms warmed up too.

Then the plumbers arrived. They fixed the plumbing, and the bathrooms started functioning properly. Nadezhda Ivanovna made a duty roaster, and the children and teachers began cleaning the building. By day five, the camp was neat and tidy.

But help continues to arrive in an endless stream, not only

from the sate but also from private donors. They've been bringing clothes, but for some strange reason only for children from eight to ten. So, the first and second graders each had about ten new t-shirts, sweaters, jackets, sneakers, and jeans, but the younger kids had nothing to wear, and the high schoolers walked around in pants barely reaching their knees and in jackets barely covering their elbows.

Nadezhda Ivanovna measured all her charges and sent their sizes to social services; they brought new clothes but again mixed up the sizes. Finally, they got everything right, and in a week's time all the children were dressed appropriately for the weather. They then asked for suitcases—to go home with all their gifts and new clothes.

To go home! Back home!

Then the ping pong tables arrived. Alexander, the resort's director and a former professional athlete suggested that they organize a ping pong championship. He was supervising the temporary constructions and wanted to keep the children occupied so they didn't get in the way. He taught the children how to make championship tables and promised that the winner would get a chance to play him in the finals. The fact that Alexander was a decorated athlete made this offer especially attractive.

The children liked this idea, and the sound of ping pong balls became the constant background noise at the resort. The children would get heated, arguing with one another, trying to prove that the ball hadn't flown off the table but touched the edge . . .

And then February 24 came, and the war began.

At first, the children didn't notice anything, but for Alexander and Nadezhda Ivanovna the changes were obvious. If during the first week of their evacuation, the donors and sponsors had provided powerful heaters, food, clothes, and ping pong tables, they were now offering to place the children with Russian families. Of course, the camp had been renovated and updated, they had organized food service, and the children were warmly dressed and attending school, but still it was camp life. The kids lived five to a room, without any of the comforts of home, so wouldn't it be better to let them live with families? Some people wanted to adopt them, while others were willing to host them for a limited amount of time. Alexander calculated that there were three times as many requests for adoption than there were children at the Stakhanov orphanage. But the Luhansk system of social services doesn't give children to families, especially to families in another country.

When the ping pong championship was nearing an end, it was time for the director to play the winner. The children gathered around the table to watch this final historic game, but Alexander had to fight back tears when he looked at the children—why are the rules created in such a way that we can't place war orphans with families of kind people with some financial means?

Alexander lost the final game—tears filled his eyes, and he could barely see the ball. After defeating the decorated athlete, the champion imposed a handicap on himself—now he would play ping pong with his friends while sitting on a chair to limit his freedom of movement and even things out.

Then the army recruiters arrived at Liski. The ping pong champion was the first to be offered admission to the Suvorov Military School. Then they invited other boys too. The kids agreed. They can't go and live with families, but it's okay for them to go to a military school. And so, there's no hope that in the near future they'll be able to return home with a suitcase full of gifts and new clothes.

Every night, after Nadezhda Ivanovna sends her charges to their rooms and makes sure they're asleep in their beds, she calls her neighbor in Stakhanov. There's news: A missile hit Nadezhda Ivanovna's house, but the walls are not damaged, only the windows are shattered. Another neighbor covered the windows with plastic wrap. The next day that neighbor was killed by a stray bullet. The orphanage is still intact, but the guard and the handyman were conscripted into the army. They were not young people—both were almost sixty, and no one knows what happened to them. And Nadezhda Ivanovna's dog, which she left with her neighbor, is always howling.

"U-u-u-u-u-u!"

"Eat, sweetie, eat."

"U-u-u-u-u-u!"

"Eat, damn it! Why are you howling as if someone died?"

Filtration

In the first days of the war, refugees from Luhansk and Kharkiv could enter Russia freely. One month later, people from Rubizhne, Izyum, and Mariupol already had to pass through filtration points. Denys D. managed to leave Mariupol by the end of March (the story of his city is coming later). They travel in two cars—Denys, his wife and children, his sister and her child, his sister's husband and their dog—and reach Berdyansk. The kids got sick, but thank God, they found some kind of resort where a refugee shelter has been organized and where they have food, medications, and a doctor. In two weeks' time, the kids will be feeling much better.

The cars are broken down, the tires are almost completely shredded on the war-damaged roads, but, thank God, Denys is an engineer who used to work at a train-car factory, and he thought to bring tools with him. While the wives take care of the sick kids, the men fix their cars.

At the beginning of April, the two families set off toward Crimea through the village of Chonhar. They wanted to go through Zaporizhzhia, through territory that's controlled by Ukraine, but the Russian armies won't let anyone go in that direction.

They take off at 6:00 A.M. To buy some gas (the price has gone up tenfold since the war began), they had to break into the kids' piggy bank. It's 237 kilometers from Berdyansk to Mostove village on the border, and there are eighteen or twenty (Denys can't remember exactly) Russian checkpoints in between. At every checkpoint, they're stopped, their documents are checked, the cars are searched, and the soldiers demand a gift—anything, even a jar of instant coffee or a pack of cigarettes. Denys doesn't smoke, but he learned about this practice from other refugees and so stocked up on coffee and cigarettes in Berdyansk. Now he passes successfully through the checkpoints.

Right before the border, there's a line of cars stretching about two kilometers. But they've set up a field kitchen and the military men provide the refugees with food and migration cards. Denys's family eats buckwheat kasha and crackers, fills out the migration forms, and waits.

At 8:00 P.M. (which means they've already been traveling for fourteen hours), it's finally their turn. They're ordered to completely unload their cars, to take everything out, even the floor mats and spare tires.

A thorough search ensues. The soldiers open all their bags and go through all their clothes. Then they carefully check their papers. The women and children get their documents back, but the men have to park their cars and go to the customs office to get their passports.

There's a room in that building, a hall of roughly sixty square meters, where about a hundred men are waiting for an interview. Some have been waiting an entire day. There's no food, no water, no bathroom. And you can't step away because you might be called at any minute. They don't call out the men in the order they arrived, it's totally random—the officer throws all their passports in a box, randomly picks one out, calls the name, and if no one answers, the passport is thrown back into the box, and who knows when they'll call you next. So, no one leaves. Everyone waits in the room with two people per square meter. There are only a few benches in the room, and the men take turns sitting.

They say if you go through the filtration camp by bus, you may end up waiting for two weeks. It's much better in your own car, but most people's cars didn't survive the shelling. They say that the filtration goes faster at night. Denys gets lucky—his name is called just three hours later, around 11:00 P.M.

He enters the room and sees two investigators. They order him to strip, keeping only his underwear on. They check him for tattoos as well as bruises typical of military men (for example, a bruise from a rifle butt on your right shoulder); they search for calluses, burns, and belt imprints typical of soldiers. Then they carefully study your cellphone. They look through all your social networks, all your photos and videos. The refugees who'd taken this route before warned Denys about the searches, and so he erased all compromising photos—photos that could possibly be connected to the war, but he kept his family photos. He erased any even remotely suspicious texts but left his private chats with his wife. That way, the phone wouldn't look empty. It would appear totally innocent and wouldn't provoke any questions. The only thing Denys forgot to erase is the number of the auto-service center where he used to take his car.

The name of the service center is Nika Azov, and that's how it's listed in his contacts.

"Who's this Nika from Azov?" the investigator asks, instantly imagining a female sniper from the Azov battalion who is hiding somewhere in the catacombs of the Severstal plant.[5]

---

[5] The Azov Battalion is a Ukrainian army division formed from volunteers in Mariupol in 2014. Originally, their goal was to fight against pro-Moscow military units participating in the effort to separate the Donetsk and Luhansk regions from Ukraine. Russian propaganda uses the Azov battalion as a symbol of so-called Ukrainian neo-Nazism.

"It's not a person," answers Denys, "it's an auto repair shop."
"Let's call your Nika."
"Okay."
No one picks up.
"Look at my car," says Denys, "there's Nika Azov on the license plate."
The inspector looks through the window, sees Denys's car, and believes him. But he keeps asking questions anyway.
"Who do you know from Azov?"
"No one."
"Have you seen how they shoot? Who was shooting?"
"No, I haven't."
"Did you see the fighters from Azov?"
"I've never seen any."
"Do you know anyone in the army?" "No, I don't know anyone."
"What about the police?"
"No one."
"Who do you know from Azov?"
"I've already said, I don't know anyone."
They repeat their questions. The investigator asks each question at least five times, and each time he asks it faster. And he adds new questions: *Has Denys served in the army? Why hasn't he served? Who do you know from Azov? And from the police? And why haven't you served? Have they made you speak Ukrainian? And who do you know from Azov? And from the police? And from the army? And why haven't you served?*

Faster and faster, they go around in circles, to confuse Denys and trip him up—and it lasts forty minutes.
"Let me go already, I have kids in the car!"
"Okay, you can go."
With his long-awaited passport in hand, Denys goes to his car, where the final test is about to begin. The car belongs to Denys's father, and Denys is driving with a motor vehicle power

of attorney, written by hand. And the customs officer knows this. The officer stays near the car and waits.

"Your car doesn't belong to you. Are you aware of that?"

"Yes, it's my father's car, and he gave me authorization."

"To cross a state border, you need an officially notarized power of attorney. Do you know that?"

"And what can I do about it now? I have kids. Do you want me to go back? I have enough gas to reach the first gas station, but there's no gas in Ukraine."

"That's your problem."

They keep talking for another half hour. This customs officer tries to extort money from Denys. First with hints, and then without beating around the bush. But they haven't got any money. Denys turns out his pockets, shows him his empty wallet. Denys's wife shows him her empty wallet too.

"Okay, go."

When Denys's car leaves the border checkpoint and enters Crimea, the clock shows 3:00 A.M. They've been on the road for twenty-one hours. His kids are sleeping. There's a banknote folded eight times in the pocket of his kid's jacket—their last hundred-dollar bill to exchange, get gas, and keep driving farther through Slavyansk-na-Kubani, Rostov, Voronezh, and Moscow—then to the West.

Dasha from Moscow

Denys drives to Kerch, then from Kerch to Slavyansk-na-Kubani, across the famous bridge. On the bridge, they're stopped and searched again. They ask some questions but let them go, without even demanding a bribe. In Slavyansk-na-Kubani, Denys manages to buy Russian SIM-cards, and from that moment on they are guided by Russian volunteers, who will lead them to the Latvian border and then pass them off to Rubikus volunteers. Dasha T., a volunteer whom Denys can call in any difficult situation, is an actress and musician, who occasionally moonlights transcribing audio transcripts for TV. Denys accepts her help with gratitude, never suspecting that Dasha's life, too, is going to hell.

In Rostov, the volunteers recruited by Dasha meet Denys, rent him an apartment for two nights, and provide him with some food and money. In the meantime, Dasha gets a call from the recruiting agency she works with. They offer her a job—transcribing interviews for the TV channel Russia Today. It's a very good gig, highly paid and long-term. But Dasha refuses the work—she doesn't want to transcribe this senseless propaganda. Those lies about the war will, of course, be published, but not with Dasha's help.

It was a surprise for the recruiting agency: "Why would you refuse such a good job?" "Do I really need to explain why?" Dasha asked.

"Well, things aren't that bad."

"No, things are indeed that bad."

Most likely the agency will never offer Dasha another job. Denys doesn't know anything about this as he sleeps in the Rostov apartment, along with his family—who are now, finally, safe and sound.

Two days later, Denys fills up his tank—an almost forgotten feeling!—and takes his family to Voronezh, where another set of Dasha's volunteers is waiting for them with a new apartment for one night and a lovingly prepared meal. Meanwhile, Dasha gets a call from her accompanist. Dasha's a jazz singer, and she can't perform without an accompanist. But her accompanist calls and says that he's leaving—he can't live in Russia anymore, he can't stand to see the letter "Z" written on all the municipal buildings and public transportation. Dasha understands and supports him, but the fact that her accompanist is leaving means that now Dasha doesn't have this job either—you can't sing jazz a cappella. Denys doesn't know anything about this. In Buturlinovka, a small city near Voronezh, he chats with the volunteers in the kitchen and can't believe there are so many kind and caring people in Russia.

The next day Denys goes to Moscow. He's stopped at every police checkpoint and his documents are checked. The highway patrol officers search him, but it's nothing personal. They even smile at him with a hint of guilt, as if to say, *Sorry, we don't have any issues with you, it's just that we have orders to check all the cars with Ukrainian license plates, so don't get upset.* Denys doesn't get upset, especially because he knows there are nice volunteers waiting for him, along with a cozy apartment, good food, and gas money. The volunteers try to convince Denys not to go straight to Latvia but to take the long way through St. Petersburg, to stay there for a time to decide where exactly to go. But Denys doesn't understand why he should take such a detour when Latvia is so close—only eight hundred kilometers, one day of driving.

"Listen, don't go to Latvia through Burachki. The checkpoint there is really bad, they pick on everyone, interrogate everyone, and search every pocket."

"Well, I don't think it can be worse than in the filtration camp."

"Listen, it's better to go through Ivangorod. There are thousands of people in Petersburg who take in refugees. You can stay there for a while, think about your future, and maybe visit the Hermitage while we look for ferry tickets and a place for you to live in Germany. And the lines are shorter at the Ivangorod checkpoint."

But Denys is reluctant to spend two extra days in Russia and drive an extra thousand kilometers in a car with a starter that's acting up. Denys decides to take a shortcut and go through Burachki. The volunteers don't argue anymore. They just write to Dasha that Denys and his family are going straight to Latvia.

The next day Dasha gets a call from the producer of a puppet theater, her third source of employment. The producer tells her the theater is closing, most of the actors are leaving for the West, but they're all going to different countries and so it won't be possible to restage their shows abroad. Dasha doesn't say anything—now she doesn't have this job either. *But it's okay*, Dasha thinks, *it's okay, I can sing in karaoke bars, in restaurants, and suburban trains.* Dasha thinks it's better for her to have a low income in Russia but do what she loves rather than have a low income in Europe and work as a supermarket cashier or a pizza delivery person.

The next morning, the GPS directs Denys down Dasha's street, and he literally drives under Dasha's windows. But Denys doesn't know that. In another ten hours, he's at the Burachki checkpoint where the line is at least two days long.

"Do you want to get through faster?" a man asks, sticking his head out of his car's window. "Give me ten thousand rubles, and your car will be tenth in line."

This is typical business in Burachki. The locals supplement their income by securing a place in line, staying there for days, and then selling their spots. In any case, Denys doesn't have ten thousand rubles; he spent his last money to buy a migration card, car insurance, which is mandatory in Latvia, and chocolate bars for the kids.

Denys is in a line that isn't moving. Dasha writes him that there's another checkpoint nearby and, according to the refugees' chatrooms, the line is much shorter. Denys drives there. There are only eight cars in this line, and it's possible to cross the border in three hours, even taking into account the fact that they'll have to completely unload the car and be searched again. They'll interrogate the kids: *What's your mommy's name? What's your daddy's name? What's your sister's name?* They take Denys to a back room and ask him questions: *Do you know the Azov steel plant? Do you know anyone in the Ukrainian police?*

The Ukrainian Army? From the Azov Battalion? And the main question, of course, is: *Who's Nika Azov? Is she a sniper?*

By nightfall, Denys with his wife and kids and his sister's family finally reach the checkpoint on the Latvian border. The officer peeks inside their cars:

"Are the kids asleep?"

"Yes, they're sleeping."

"It's okay, don't wake them up."

As soon as the officer stamps their passports, they are free to go. The Rubikus volunteers are already here. They have found a house in Latvia where Denys's family can stay overnight, and they have booked them tickets for the ferry from Liepāja to Hamburg. In Hamburg, they place Denys with his wife and children in a small but comfortable apartment in a multi-storey building. Denys gets 1600 euro per month in assistance for his immediate family, but for some time he has a problem spending the money—every day his neighbors bring them food and clothes and take turns inviting them for lunch and dinner.

Denys cherishes the memories of the volunteers who helped him in Russia and tells his new German neighbors all about them, explaining passionately that not all Russians are cruel bribetakers who are armed-to-the-teeth. There are selfless people among them as well. He doesn't say anything about Dasha who brought all these volunteers together. He simply doesn't know that she exists.

And Dasha stays in Russia and continues helping refugees from Ukraine travel through Russia to the West. She doesn't want to emigrate. She prefers that the so-called patriots who wear the letter "Z" on their clothes hate her for denouncing the war and helping refugees evacuate—at least they hate her for something she really believes in. It's better than to be hated in Europe for being Russian and for starting this war—for something she's not guilty of.

"Nazi Collaborators"

There are several thousand volunteers in Russia, and there's always someone on call, ready to help the refugees at any time, day or night, along their long journey from Taganrog to Petersburg.

They take in the refugees, allowing them to stay overnight at their apartments—in thousands of apartments. They spend their own money—hundreds of thousands of rubles—to pay for the refugees' gas, train and bus tickets, phones, and food. They cook cutlets for the refugees and fix their cars; they buy winter boots, medication, wheelchairs, and carriers for their cats—and they do all this anonymously.

These volunteers don't break any laws. In Russia, where it's prohibited to even say "the war," there's no law that prohibits helping refugees get where they want to go.

In the chatroom, they don't use their real names, only nicknames, and the people don't personally know one another. Just in case, they avoid any conversations about politics or the war—they're afraid of being charged under the law against public defamation of the military (which carries a sentence of up to twenty years in prison). In short, they exercise extreme caution. Which still doesn't completely protect them from snitches.

Despite this secrecy, there are already a few victims among the Rubikus volunteers who have been prosecuted for their humanitarian activity. The story of two volunteers from Penza—the economist Irina Gurskaya and the lawyer Igor Zhulimov—is the most representative.

There's a refugee camp in the Village of Leonidovka near Penza. The Ukrainian authorities call it a concentration camp and insist that the refugees are kept there by force. That's not exactly true. Leonidovka is a former camp for shift workers, a whole settlement of red-roofed barracks. Several years ago, soldiers lived there while working on the destruction of chemical weapons. Once the chemical weapons had been destroyed, or better concealed, the barracks were no longer occupied.

In April 2022, almost fifteen hundred refugees, mainly from Mariupol, were brought to the barracks in Leonidovka. No one held them there by force. About a third of the refugees were happy with the living conditions in Leonidovka and were saying that, judging by their communications with friends and relatives who had emigrated to the West, the Penza barracks were more comfortable than Polish shopping centers or German gyms, where refugees had to sleep on the floor at night and remove the mattresses during the day. In Leonidovka, they were allowed to lie down all day long.

The other two thirds wanted to leave, but all their money was in *hryvnias* and there was no free transportation for refugees in Russia. No one was detaining them, but they couldn't leave. People expressed their dissatisfaction, but they didn't rebel.

The Penza priest Father Vladimir Ketane hoped to alleviate the refugees' concerns with humanitarian aid and peaceful sermons and to switch their minds away from conversations such as: "You attacked us, and now you don't even let us leave." But the sermons didn't help, and the discontent grew.

At this point, Irina Gurskaya and Igor Zhulimov began an online fundraising campaign to buy train tickets to send refugees through Petersburg to Narva where the Rubikus volunteers would meet them and guide them through Europe. Nothing illegal was being done. Nevertheless, pro-government Telegram channels labelled Gurskaya and Zhulimov "British grant-suckers" who "live according to Bandera printouts" and "support fake news about Russian concentration camps."

An unidentified person wrote in blue and yellow paint on Igor Zhulimov's apartment door: "Ukrainian nationalist lives here." The same caption appeared on the door of Irina Gurskaya's apartment. The next day, someone punctured the tires of Igor

Zhulimov's car, and the police arrested Irina Gurskaya on the pretense of an anonymous report. Gurskaya was interrogated for almost an entire day—first, in a police department, then unknown people in masks drove her to the woods where they tried to scare her; they beat her up and then detonated a sound bomb above her head . . .

The main object of the interrogation was Gurskaya's cellphone, which the people in masks combed through looking for traces of foreign financing and inquiring about the people who communicated with her about the refugees. It's good that Gurskaya truly didn't know any of them personally, only by their nicknames. In twenty-four hours, they let Gurskaya go, but they kept her papers, including her passport.

Zhulimov wrote on social media that he's ending his volunteer work helping refugees evacuate to the West because "the business took a dangerous turn."

Gurskaya's friends took her to Moscow and hid her there. Human rights activists helped Gurskaya request new documents, obtain a visa remotely to a European country, and leave Russia.

In total, Zhulimov and Gurskaya helped thirty-eight people leave Leonidovka. Thirty-eight refugees out of fifteen hundred.

One of the evacuated families, by the way, established a fun tradition. When passing through St. Petersburg, where refugees usually spend a couple of days, they went to the Neva embankment and took a selfie with the Cruiser Aurora in the background. And when they cross the border, when they're already in Estonia, they post that picture on social media with the hashtag "Russian warship, go fuck yourself!"

Chapter 7
Children of War

"In honor of the birthday of the poet Mikhail Matusovsky, groups from Russia, Lugansk, Donets, and Kherson performed the song 'Where My Motherland Begins.' 'Where My Motherland Begins' is a song that was known by all the children of Russia and the former countries of the Soviet Union. The song was written by Matusovsky, a native of Lugansk, whose birthday is celebrated on July 23. Mikhail Matusovsky and the song 'Where My Motherland Begins' are a bridge forever connecting our people and our nations." Official Telegram Channel of the Russian Ministry of Defense, July 23, 2022.

A Robot Left Behind

Denys D. believes that his main achievement has been to save the children. By protecting them physically, the children survived—they weren't killed or injured. It's terrible, but according to data provided by the Attorney General of Ukraine, 232 children died in the first three months of the war. Another 431 children were injured. With some rounding off, it means that every day of the war takes the lives of three children and cripples five.

The volunteers discuss one of the tasks they tried to accomplish. The Baby Jesus Pediatric Hospital in Milan asked them to help find Cyrillic workbooks for writing with the non-dominant hand. In other words, a child who learned how to write with his right hand suddenly has to learn how to write with his left hand. Or the reverse—a kid used to be left-handed, but circumstances have made him right-handed. What kind of circumstances, you ask? Or have you already guessed? Yes, a hand was amputated. It could have been a shrapnel injury, a wound left unattended, gangrene ... It's impossible to believe, but the refugees insist it happened. "It happened! He grabbed a mine disguised as a toy on the ground." Personally, I refuse to believe in toy-bombs and believe that Russian infiltrators may have intentionally planted them on the street. I haven't personally seen a child who's been injured in this way, but it's quite enough that injured children sat in basements for weeks, that humanitarian corridors for their evacuation weren't opened, and that there was no medical help available, and no medications.

Add to the number of injured children, those who didn't receive the necessary medical help. Remember, in the beginning of this book I wrote that on the second day of the war in the Kyiv hospital Okhmatdet a fifteen-year-old girl underwent a bone marrow transplant to treat leukemia. But then these surgeries stopped. What happened to those children who needed transplants but never received them? Were they evacuated to Germany and treated there? Or did they die and never make it into the Attorney General's statistics? I haven't found any answers.

The only thing I do know is that a woman from Mariupol asked the Russian charitable organization Rusfond (with whom I had the honor to work) for help. Her five-year-old daughter had severe scoliosis. The girl needs to wear a special corset that has to be changed at least once a year as she grows. Her corsets used to be made in a special clinic in Kharkiv. This March it was time to change the corset again, but the war began. For two months, mother and daughter hid from the bombing in the basement. During that time, the clinic in Kharkiv ceased to exist, all the doctors left, and, in any case, you couldn't reach it through the line of fire. During those two months in the bomb shelter, the girl lost a lot of weight, becoming almost dystrophic, so she could only use her old corset for a bit longer. Then the Rusfond bought her a new one.

Finally, we must admit, practically all the children, at least all the child refugees that I know, have gotten sick with severe respiratory illnesses either in the bomb shelters or on the evacuation routes. Compared to amputated limbs or interrupted chemotherapy, this, of course, is nothing, but what would you say if in peacetime some politician contaminated several million kids with pneumonia with a single stroke of his pen?

In any case, when Denys D. says, "I was able to save my children," he's referring not only to their physical state but also to their psychological wellbeing. True, over the course of their long flight the children had occasionally been hungry, scared, and had cried a lot. True, they'd driven under bombing in a car full of suitcases and blankets that were supposed to protect them from a stray bullet or a shard of shrapnel. But then they reached Hamburg, had plenty to eat and a lot of rest, and the children felt safe again. And very soon, in a week perhaps, the kids were already running around and having fun, and everyone could hear their cheerful chatter in Ukrainian and Russian on German playgrounds.

True, but not true. Negative feelings evoked by evacuation can deeply affect children. Some of the circumstances of their escape that might seem meaningless to adults can really torture a child over weeks and months, and any child psychologist will tell you that such trauma should be taken very seriously.

Yuri and Karina Kovalchuk's five-year-old son, for instance, made a tragic mistake when he was fleeing Kyiv. His mom was rushing around, packing their bags, and she let him take only one toy with him. Without thinking, the little boy took the toy he was playing with at that moment—a dinosaur. And his beloved robot was left behind. The boy even remembers where: in the middle of the room, near the door that leads to the entryway. Psychologist Anastasiya Ryazanova, who works with children at the Communication Space Center in Moscow, says that a favorite toy is a transitional object, a security blanket, if you will. When a child discovers that there are other people in the world besides his parents and that he can and should build relationships with them, his favorite toy plays the role of a mediator. A mediator guarantees safety. The loss of a mediator, therefore, takes away that feeling of security. It's usually not so bad during the day. The boy is distracted, playing with the toys he received from donors and host families. Every day, the boy goes to the zoo, because it's nearby and a refugee's ticket is only five euros (a regular ticket is 65 euros). But at night when he goes to sleep and closes his eyes, the little boy sees his beloved robot—Did you have a favorite toy when you were a kid?—standing in the middle of the room, close to the door that leads to the entryway.

At first, Yuri and Karina didn't worry too much over the fact that every night their little boy buries his face in his pillow and weeps softly over his lost robot. They would tell him, "Wait, we'll get assistance money and buy you a new robot, an even better one." Then they realized that it's more serious than that: It's about lost love, the betrayal of a friend, and an unforgettable feeling of guilt—*I left him behind! I abandoned him!* So, every night, the parents tell their son fairytales about his robot. Actually, the robot was not forgotten—he chose to stay in Kyiv in the empty apartment to protect our home. And to water our flowers, to dust the furniture, and to keep its eye on the other toys. And to wait for his little boy to come home. *You'll return, and the robot will be waiting for you at the door that leads from the living room to the entryway.*

The boy demands these robot fairytales every day, and it seems to be helping. But if I were in Yuri and Karina's shoes, I'd go further. I would find exactly the same robot, rub him with sand so it looked like a real refugee who had suffered under bombing and during evacuation. Then for about five days I would tell the boy that the robot is on his way. One day he'd arrive in Lviv, then in Przemysl, Berlin, and Cologne. I would tell the boy how the Rubikus volunteers led the robot through Europe, how they booked him hostels to stay overnight and then train tickets for the next leg of his trip. And eventually the robot would arrive.

That's what I would've done. But the psychologist Anastasiya Ryazanova believes it's a dangerous idea. It's not that simple to deceive a child. With some kids, this trick might work, but some will see through the lie. It's better to treat the loss of a transitional object, a favorite toy, as you would deal with the loss of a person close to the child. Ryazanova says it's better to write a letter to the robot and tell him about their news, about their new life in Cologne. Then put the letter in an envelope along with some photos and drawings, seal the letter and send it to Kyiv through mail.

To Freeze or Flee

Describing the Vienna Center for Refugees, Katya L. discusses two categories of children she's met over there—those who stay still and those who run. Katya says that before the war she'd never seen a five-year-old who could stay in one spot for forty-five minutes without moving, staring at a single spot, and without something in his hands to fiddle with. Here in Vienna, she's seen many cases like that.

A family approaches Katya—a mother, a grandmother, and a boy of five. Katya asks the usual questions: name, age, any chronic diseases—while the boy stands there with his shoulder blades barely touching the wall; he's motionless like a statue. *Do you have pets? Do you have a working cellphone?* And the boy is immobile, frozen. He might be breathing but it's difficult to detect whether his chest and stomach are moving.

"Sweetie, what's your name?"

No answer.

"Do you want to see our kids' corner? There's a lot of toys."

No answer.

"We have people here who will play with you. They can draw with you too. Let's go? Do you want your mom to take you there?"

The boy remains silent.

This is an ancient animal reaction to danger—to freeze, play dead. Many animals do this instinctually, hoping that predators won't eat a victim they didn't kill themselves. In this sense, the war takes children back twenty million years, not to the pre-Neanderthal period but to our pre-simian past, to the time when we were frogs, gerbils, amoebas.

It's interesting that the parents are okay with their children being in such a state. They don't try to shake them out of it or to entertain them. It's convenient for an exhausted mother to take a kid to the Refugee Center, put him next to the wall, and then respond absent-mindedly to the volunteers' questions—name, age, any chronic diseases, phone, car . . .

With children who run around, the situation is more complicated. A mother exhausted by bomb shelters and evacuation routes sits at Katya L.'s desk, but she doesn't really answer her questions. Instead, swaying slightly, she says in a quiet voice: "Catch my daughter. Someone catch my daughter. Please. I can't catch her."

Katya looks around. Just a second ago, there was a girl standing on the left side of her desk. And now the girl is gone. Katya gets up. The Refugee Center is big—it used to be a sports complex before the war. The girl is nowhere to be seen. Oh, no, there she is—running, dodging like a hare among the families of refugees, the volunteers' desks, and the boxes of humanitarian food and clothes. Katya is a grownup woman. She can't run that fast and maneuver so skillfully around the boxes. So, she yells: "Stop that girl, please!"

One of the volunteers hears her and squats in front of the runaway—almost all the volunteers are students majoring in psychology, and they know that it's essential to be on the same level as the child and to make eye contact. But no luck, the girl escapes, dives under the desk, and then keeps running. Now the entire Center is trying to catch her, and knowledge of human psychology is of no use—we're dealing with animal psychology here. It's the most primordial instinct—run!

On the second or third day of her shift at the Vienna Refugee Center, Katya comes up with a solution, instinctively for that matter. She decides to hug the "frozen" children and quietly tell them some stories, "Once upon a time, there was a boy, and that boy had a friend, a puppy . . . " To the "running" children, Katya offers to jump. She holds hands with a kid—a grownup woman and a girl of about seven—and they start jumping, until the animal instinct leaves the child and the human capacity to think returns.

Ekaterina Kadieva owns a private school in France, a fairly expensive school. And she also has another school in Turkey—more democratic, called Dialogue, and designed for Russian and Ukrainian children who don't know any English, or don't know it very well. The school's goal is to help children become proficient in English, adapt to modern European teaching methods, and then move on to the high school of their choice. Many European and American high schools gladly accept Dialogue graduates, even for free.

With a tuition of only ten thousand euros a year, Dialogue can certainly be considered a democratic school. For emigrants from Russia—computer programmers, businessmen, and intellectuals that refuse to live in a country that has started and promoted a war—such tuition is affordable. For refugees from Ukraine—it's not.

To make studying at Dialogue available to all refugees, Boris Zimin, a businessman and the son of the philanthropist Dmitry Borisovich Zimin, established twenty scholarships. A few scholarships came from the wealthy parents of other Dialogue students, and several more were sponsored by Kadieva herself, from the French school's profits. That's how Ukrainian children came to be at Dialogue.

But Ekaterina Kadieva says they've forgotten how to sleep. Post-traumatic stress disorder makes the child refugees easily disturbed by any sharp sound. If, let's say, a cook drops a lid on the stone floor of the kitchen, the children from Ukraine are startled and start looking around to figure out where the sound came from. It's also hard for them to fully understand jokes—any comment from their classmates they perceive as an insult, any prank they perceive as mean-spirited. And they often complain of phantom pains—headaches, stomach aches, pain in their legs. These aches usually go away after their sessions with the psychologists, not from medication.

The main health problem for these children is that they can't sleep. Some students even try not to change into their pajamas at night and go to bed fully dressed and lie not underneath but on top of their comforters. As if they're preparing to jump up and run at the first alarming sound in the night. And because they don't get enough sleep, it's hard for them to study during the day.

On the other hand, Kadieva admits that, aside from the PTSD, the child refugees have learned amazing tolerance and wisdom from their traumatic experience. The PTSD will pass, but the wisdom will remain.

For instance, a Ukrainian girl and a Russian boy met at school. To leave Ukraine, the girl had stood at the Polish border for six hours in the snow. The boy, on the other hand, had been woken up by his parents early in the morning on February 24, put in their car, and driven away from Moscow. When they met, the boy and girl treated each other with surprising care, as if realizing they'd experienced the same hardship. I imagine the adults, both Russians and Ukrainians, won't be able to act like this for many years to come. I hope the children will.

The Peculiarities of Memory

The memory of children who have experienced at least several days of war undergoes the most amazing transformations. They remember things that never happened and don't remember what actually did happen. Or, from among all the misfortunes a little kid has endured, his or her memory picks out only one particular episode, one specific detail, and remembers it vividly while erasing the rest. Incidentally, wartime memory works selectively for adults as well.

Vladimir Pavlenko—remember, the blinds and curtains salesman from Odesa?—installed two apps on his phone in the first days of the war. The first app was a local radio station for air raid alerts, while the second was advice from psychologists. All psychologists were adamant in their recommendations to parents to spend as much time as possible with their children. Play with them, hold them, hug them, try to talk to them, and by no means leave them alone playing soulless games on their phones with the thunder of bombs all around them.

Vladimir remembers that he took that advise seriously and played with his daughter for entire days. It was unusual because during peace time, Daddy spent the day at work and was home only in the evening. But during the war father and daughter played from morning to night. They played all the time, but it's very strange that Vladimir can't remember what games they played. Was it Peek-a-Boo? Hide and seek? Did they play with dolls? In response to my question about the games, Vladimir rubs his forehead intensely, wrinkles his brow, and shrugs his shoulders in bewilderment: "I don't remember."

Vladimir's daughter, on the other hand, remembers that Daddy played with her very little. This is probably what happened: Before the war, they didn't play together at all, and when the war started, the little girl was so shocked by this new possibility that she wanted to play with her dad more and more. But there are only twenty-four hours in a day, and at some point, it became impossible to increase her playtime with Daddy, and that is what stuck in the girl's mind—Daddy refuses to play.

At the Vienna Center for Refugees, a seven-year-old boy insists to Katya L. that they didn't experience any bombing. This boy is from Kharkiv, where they were bombed for days on end—just open the air raid alert app and you'll see that Kharkiv was bombed twenty times a day. But the little boy insisted: *No, there were no planes flying above our heads, and we weren't bombed.* And, as if to prove his point, he'd take a used machine-gun shell from his pocket: *Look what I've found—a treasure.* From a thousand used shells on the road, he picks up one and keeps it as if concentrating his entire memory on the object. And erasing everything else from his mind.

In Munich, a refugee girl from Kyiv tells Alya Khaitlina and the other volunteers that she loves the birds in Germany. There are indeed many interesting birds in Bavaria, but it's not the Amazon jungle—there aren't parrots and toucans flying out of the trees. But the girl insists: The birds are special here, there aren't any birds like that in Kyiv. At every opportunity, the little girl would talk about the birds—obviously, it was very important to her.

A volunteer psychologist decided to find out what the big difference was between the sparrows and pigeons in Munich and those in Kyiv. The girl was happy to explain: Here in Munich, the birds don't fall to one side while they're flying, they don't fly in circles, like insects around a lamp, they don't crash into lampposts and trees, and they don't flounder around on the ground with their legs in the air. But that's what the birds do in Kyiv—they fall to the side, fly in circles, crash into things, and flounder on the ground.

Here's another image of war for you—injured birds, flocks of injured birds. Among the hundreds of refugees I talked with, no one ever mentioned the birds, but this young girl noticed only them, her memory focused on that image.

Despite the strong opinion of many psychologists, I'd like to believe that cellphones don't further damage a mind already disturbed by the war but can actually help a child survive. Children appear to delegate a part of their mind to the cellphone—it's made from steel, and its microchips won't be destroyed by fear, not like human nerve cells. Alla Achasova remembers that in their family, her youngest son was the least afraid. Before they made it to Czechia, he was glued to his phone for three entire weeks playing a game where some monsters known only to children shoot at one other. In his mind, the real shooting outside got somehow mixed up with the virtual gunfire on his phone, and the real monsters attacking Kharkiv seemed no more dangerous than their virtual counterparts.

Victoria Svetlich is convinced that the phone was her daughter's salvation. At first, the girl only cried when she looked at her phone, where her previous life still existed, if only in virtual form. School continued virtually through Zoom, and the kids could chat with their classmates over the breaks. The girl's boyfriend (her first) evacuated with his parents along a different route, but they could always chat with each other on social networks or play the same videogame together, a game they used to play with their heads touching. The girl didn't delete the air-raid alarm app on her phone. Victoria was already driving along safe European roads when the air-raid siren would suddenly go off on her daughter's phone. Startled, Victoria would instinctively look around in search of approaching bombers.

"Will you delete that app already?"

"No, mama, I won't!"

By the way, many refugees now living in peaceful German, Dutch, and French towns and cities still keep the air-raid-alarm app on their phones. As if the howl of that air-raid alarm somehow connects them with the people back home.

A Tankman's Brother

Danya is screaming. Nadezhda Ivanovna can't immediately figure out what that sound in the darkness is—an animal-like howl and a dull crashing noise. Actually, no, at first Nadezhda Ivanovna thinks that the howl and the crashing are coming from her phone—the one she uses to call her neighbor in Stakhanov. It takes her several seconds to realize that the scary sound is somewhere here, in the dark hallway of the second floor of their summer camp in Liski, where the orphans under her care are now living.

Nadezhda Ivanovna runs toward the sound. The staircase is dark. They haven't lived here long enough for her to remember automatically where the light switches are. The second-floor hallway is dark too. And there's a shadow in the hallway that howls and bangs against the wall—it falls down on the ping pong table, jumps up, runs, and bangs against the wall.

Suddenly the lights are on. It's Alexander, the camp director, who truly knows where all the switches are because he's spent the entire day fixing them, and now he's here too, awakened by the noise.

The hallway is now illuminated, but it would have probably been better if it weren't. Nadezhda Ivanovna sees Danya, a boy of about twelve. His face is bright red, as if someone ripped off his skin, and it's distorted by despair. There's blood on his hands and clothes. There are inarticulate noises coming from the boy's wide-open mouth:

"Olya! I'll ill'em! I'll oot'em!" The boy screams and falls again on the ping pong table, then jumps up, runs, and bangs into the wall.

The other teachers who had come with the children from Stakhanov run toward the screaming. Five women somehow manage to catch the boy and press themselves against him. And that's how they're standing, in a tight circle with Danya throbbing in the middle:

"Olya! I'll ill'em! I'll oot'em!"

The t-shirts of the five teachers are wet with Danya's tears and blood. Gradually, Danya calms down. His screaming subsides to a whisper. The words he's saying are clearer now: "Kolya! I'll kill them! I'll shoot them!"

Nadezhda Ivanovna knows (everyone knows everyone in Stakhanov) that Kolya is Danya's eighteen-year-old brother, his only close relation on Earth. Kolya was studying to become a mechanic and used to visit often, bringing gifts and candy for his younger brother. He promised that as soon as he gets a job and finishes his service in the army, he'll take Danya away from the orphanage, and they'll live together. Kolya will work, and Danya will go to school. And Nadezhda Ivanovna will help them both with her advice.

The last time Kolya came to visit his brother, he was wearing a tankman's uniform—not even a new one, a hand-me-down probably. Then the Stakhanov orphanage was evacuated to Voronezh, and since then there's been no news of Kolya. News must have arrived.

Nadezhda Ivanovna looks around and sees Danya's cellphone on the floor. The screen is broken, but it shows the last call was from the boy's Aunt Rita. Nadezhda Ivanovna knows her too—she's Danya's distant relative, a second cousin twice removed or maybe the grandmother of Danya's mother who disappeared without a trace and whose parental rights had been suspended.

Nadezhda Ivanovna calls her back and, while waiting for someone to pick up, thinks: *Maybe he's just injured?*

No, he's been killed.

Aunt Rita is sobbing on the phone:

"They killed our Kolya!"

And all Nadezhda Ivanovna can say in return:

"What an idiot you are! Couldn't you tell that to some adults first? How could you dump all that on a little boy?!"

The next afternoon, Aunt Rita's husband calls on Danya's cellphone. That morning, Nadezhda Ivanovna and Danya made a deal that the boy wouldn't answer his phone anymore. No matter who was calling, Nadezhda Ivanovna would talk to them first. Aunt Rita's husband, it seems, is not entirely sober, but he sounds like a nice guy. Nadezhda Ivanovna thinks it's better for the boy to have not-always sober relatives than to have no relatives at all and gives the boy the phone. She also puts the phone on speaker. The uncle, or maybe he's the second cousin twice removed, expresses his condolences and then tells the boy not to worry, the Russians don't leave their own behind. And Danya won't be left behind, not by his second cousins many-time removed, and not by the authorities of the Luhansk People's Republic. Then the uncle gets too drunk or maybe too excited and begins telling the orphan stories about the glorious military traditions of his family. How his great-grandfather fought in the Battle of Kursk. How his other great-grandfather stormed Budapest. How after the WWII, everyone looked after everyone, and everyone was a Hero of Socialist Labor.

At this point Nadezhda Ivanovna loses her temper, takes Danya's phone from him, and then takes a step away so the boy won't hear. She says:

"If there are such glorious military traditions in your family, how could you put a little boy in an orphanage?"

The man is embarrassed for a moment, but then responds forcefully, with a challenge:

"I'll take him. I thought Kolya would take him, but know I'll take him. As soon as the war is over, I'll take him. What do I have to do? Write an official request? I'll do that."

Nadezhda Ivanovna hangs up because she can tell by his voice the man is lying.

Several days later, Danya asks the officers who came to recruit for the Suvorov Military School:

"Can I become a tankman when I finish the Suvorov School?"

"Of course, you can. You can go into any branch you choose if your health allows," the officer answers and adds Danya's name to the preliminary list of recruits, which will need to be approved by the Ministry of Social Affairs and Education of the Luhansk Republic. But it's not likely he'll be rejected. It seems to be the family's fate—the glorious military tradition of dying in tanks will erase this family completely.

Roman and Yulia

Yulia is fourteen, and Roman is seventeen. Yulia left Ukraine with her grandfather, who's over eighty. The Rubikus volunteers assumed, quite logically, that Yulia was responsible for her grandfather, not the reverse, and were helping them from bus to bus and from hostel to hostel. The grandfather had no idea how to communicate with the volunteers in the chatrooms, how to use GPS, or how to open maps and public transportation schedules on his phone. He didn't even know how to pay with his bank card, even though he did have a bank card and there was some money on it. Before the war, the old man would just go to the bank and withdraw some cash from his account. On their journey, when Yulia didn't communicate with the volunteers through the chatroom but talked with them on the phone, the grandfather would ask her to give him the phone and then say:

"Don't worry, I'm keeping an eye on the young people over here," and with this reassurance, his participation in the logistics came to an end. This was how Yulia and her grandpa made it to Riga.

Roman had already begun living in Riga. With the Rubikus volunteers, he completed the entire evacuation route, settled temporarily in the Latvian capital, and became a volunteer himself. His job was to meet the so-called Northern Stream refugees (the people who were coming to Europe from Russia), help them settle in the fifty-room local hostel that Rubikus rented in Riga, and accompany the refugees to the ferry for Tallinn or Helsinki, where they would then take trains to Stockholm or Copenhagen.

Roman and Yulia didn't meet at a ball; they met at a bus station. They didn't talk about love on a balcony under the mysterious moon; they opened their hearts in the tiny kitchen of a noisy overpopulated hostel. In the early morning, Roman would leave his beloved not because the larks began singing but because people were crowding into the kitchen to prepare food and he had to get up early the next day to see Yulia and her grandpa off to the ferry. But one thing happened just like in Shakespeare: Their eyes met, and they fell in love. And now the grandfather, who truly didn't have anything to do but keep an eye on the young people, noticed their affection and started to complain. For the first time since their evacuation began, he called the Rubikus volunteers himself and said that something was not right here in Europe—something very sinister was happening. Some young guy was following his under-aged granddaughter, and since he couldn't get rid of this guy, they don't need any volunteers to see them off—they aren't children, and they can find their way around by themselves. You can't miss the sea anyway, and the ferry is huge, like a building, you can see it for miles. In short, take this volunteer guy away from them before he corrupts his granddaughter. But the worst that could happen would be that the young man comes in the morning, takes Yulia's suitcase in his right hand, and with his left hand secretly holds Yulia's hand. For half the night Yulia and the Rubikus volunteers, who normally try to reassure the refugees that everything will be fine, tried to reason with the grandfather by telling him that it's impossible to navigate through Riga without a guide. They told him that the Latvian language is extremely complicated while forgetting to mention that almost everyone in Riga can speak Russian. They were saying how difficult the public transportation is in Riga, lied to him, telling him that the same number trams and buses could go in different directions and that you can't figure it out without special knowledge.

By fair means or foul, by morning they'd managed to convince the old man to allow Roman to be their volunteer. And the young lovers managed to sneak in a few handshakes, friend each other on social media, and even hold each other's hands secretly for a little while, even though the grandpa was dutifully keeping an eye on them.

In the Rubikus chatroom, where idle chatting is frowned upon and only business-related posts are welcome, this story became very popular and was discussed with great passion. People that fall in love are always discussed with special awe, and the volunteers try to help them stay together. I think I understand why it happens. People are wired to believe that from the irreconcilable hatred of adults the sacred love of young people can emerge. The kind of love that inspires songs and legends. One of the best poems by the Russian poet Alya Khaitlina who now lives in Germany is about such love.

That poem is about the wedding of a very young couple, almost children, that takes place in the Azovstal plant's basement under shelling. There was a wise man in that basement—a senior officer or retired judge, who convinced the couple that he had the right to officiate their marriage under these dire circumstances, and to overlook the fact that the bride-to-be was underage. They made rings from tin cans. They signed a soiled piece of paper that served as their marriage certificate. Everyone brought whatever food they had, and the wedding reception took place under bombardment. One of the guests who could imitate the sounds of a saxophone "played" a waltz. While the

"saxophone" was playing, the bride and groom danced their first dance in the shadows of a bomb shelter.
Two weeks before summer in a half-lit basement,
He whispered in her ear, "I've loved you since we were kids."
"You're stepping on my foot," she told him.
And then a missile reached its target. They perished together.

Chapter 8
The War and Aids

> "During the special military operation, documents were seized indicating that, since 2019, USAID and its main contractor, the company Labyrinth Ukraine, have been taking part in a biological warfare program of the US military. The command of the Ukrainian Armed Forces has declared its willingness to cooperate with USAID in injecting military personnel with vaccines and in collecting, processing and passing on information of interest to the Americans." Head of the Radiation, Chemical and Biological Defense Division of the Armed Forces of the Russian Federation, Lieutenant General Igor Kirillov, August 4, 2022.

A Challenging Passenger

Alexandra Volgina wakes up in her rental apartment in Amsterdam. First thing in the morning, before making coffee for herself and breakfast for her children, she checks her phone. There are black avatars all over the social networks—Sasha's Ukrainian friends are in mourning. "Damn it! Now what's happened? Can things really get any worse?"

It's been a week since the war began. Sasha and her older daughter are Russian citizens, but Sasha's husband and their younger daughter are Ukrainians. For an entire week, the country that two members of this family call their own has been destroying the homeland of the other two members of that family. Sasha's husband packed his bag, bought a bulletproof vest, and went to fight for Ukraine. If Sasha could have, she would have followed him. Her grandmother is from Chernigov, and the city's been bombed. As a kid, Sasha spent every summer in a place that Russian missiles are now trying to destroy. But for Sasha, this war has been going on much longer—not a week, and not even the eight years the Donetsk and Luhansk regions have been trying to separate from Ukraine. This war is driving Sasha to despair, but it came as no surprise. Everyone is trying to find the answer to the question: "How can Russia kill totally innocent people?" But Sasha knows that Russia can kill. Russia has already killed innocent people in Chechnya, Syria, the school in Beslan, in the Moscow theater . . . Moreover, for many years Russia has been killing Sasha herself and her friends. So, by now Sasha feels like she knows how to survive and how to help others survive too.

Sasha has AIDS and three types of hepatitis. In the last century, at the end of the 90s, when Sasha was very young, she was living in Petersburg and using drugs, like many other young people were doing at the time. She contracted AIDS by sharing needles—and she was totally ignorant about the virus. After four years of doing drugs, on the verge of death, Sasha quit and became one of the first Russian activists to demand that the state treat people with AIDS just as they treat people with high blood pressure or diabetes.

In Russia at the beginning of the twenty-first century, there were no drugs to treat AIDS. Sasha and her friends chained themselves with handcuffs to the doors of the Ministry of Health and demanded they provide those infected with the medications they needed. They chanted: "Our death is your shame!" The protesters would be arrested and put in jail, but as soon as they were released, they would continue the fight.

At the same time, they founded several social groups to help one another. Sasha, for instance, organized a community of HIV-infected people in Petersburg and named it *Svecha*, or candle. *Svecha* activists took care of the dying, explained to those who were infected how to live with the virus, taught others how to avoid getting infected, supported harm reduction programs, and tried to convince pharmaceutical companies to make AIDS treatments more affordable. In short, they tried to stop the epidemic the state was ignoring.

There was a moment when it seemed that common sense was winning. President Putin signed a decree declaring that those infected with HIV were not monsters who were destined to perish, but human beings who deserved to be treated. After that, the first anti-AIDS drugs arrived in Russia. Global HIV/AIDS organizations were legally allowed on Russian territory, and small local groups, like *Svecha*, joined global initiatives, which allowed them to implement state-of-the-art medical treatments and social programs to halt the epidemic. But such good fortune didn't last.

The more regressive the Russian government has become, the more undesirable and abnormal it deemed modern social programs. *Reduce harm? Give away clean syringes to people doing drugs? No way!* the Russian authorities would scream, and they banned such programs. *Protect sex-workers and other vulnerable population groups? Care for them? No way!*—and they banned those programs too. *Substitution therapy? Provide methadone to heroin addicts? Never! Public educational campaigns? No way! Sex-education in primary schools? How immoral! They'll corrupt innocent minds! It's the pernicious influence of the West! NO, NO, and NO!*

Sasha moved to Kyiv to develop medical and social support services for HIV-infected people within the broader post-Soviet space. In Kyiv, there were good things and bad. On the one hand, there was the fragrant summer air, a new love, romantic dates in Pechersk in the tiny apartment of her future husband, then marriage and the birth of her younger daughter. On the other hand, there was the government corruption under President Yanukovych . . .

Then the Revolution of Dignity happened. From November 2013 to February 2014, during the Maidan Uprising, the office of the Kyiv Center for HIV-infected People became a field hospital. Sasha took care of the injured.

While the corruption didn't disappear in the wake of the

successful revolution, it decreased significantly. Civil society was developing under the motto "Let's do as Europe does!" Modern social technologies for HIV prevention were being implemented. Harm reduction programs, methadone replacement therapy, public information campaigns, and sex education in schools were initiated, and the epidemic began to subside.

Just look at the statistics to see how democracy helps fight this epidemic. In Ukraine, the epidemic stabilized and infection rates began to decrease, while in Russia, the numbers were increasing exponentially. Just compare the numbers: In Russia, 58% of HIV-positive patients receive antiretroviral therapy; in Ukraine—83%. Among HIV-positive people who take their medications regularly, 80% of those in Russia reached an undetectable viral load, which means they can't infect anyone through sexual contact, while in Ukraine it is 93%. The numbers in Russia and Ukraine were, however, the same before the Revolution of Dignity. This means that in Ukraine organizations for HIV-positive people have been successful in promoting patient adherence to treatment regimens. In Russia, Alexandra Volgina's *Svecha* fund and other programs for HIV patients are now defined as foreign agents and have been closed. That's why people are dying—the state is killing them by refusing to see them as human beings.

There was another time the Russian state attempted to kill Sasha. On July 17, 2014, she was going to fly to an international conference in Australia. She was traveling from Amsterdam to Kuala Lumpur on Malaysian Airline flight MN-17. But right before her trip, Sasha had a seminar in Vilnius, and if she went directly to Australia from there, she wouldn't see her daughter for an entire month. So, Sasha asked to change her ticket so she could go to Kyiv for one day to see her daughter. They changed her ticket.

Sasha flew to Kyiv and turned off her phone so that, for the next twenty-four hours, she'd receive no calls or social media alerts, and she could concentrate completely on her daughter. Meanwhile in the airspace over the Donbas region, a Russian Buk missile hit the Boeing MN-17—the plane that Sasha was initially booked on. Among the two hundred ninety-eight passengers and crew members who died in that catastrophe was the Dutch doctor Joep Lange who developed the method to prevent the vertical transmission of HIV, from mother to child. Thanks to that method, HIV-positive Sasha was able to give birth to two healthy daughters. Joep Lange was flying with his four children. Sasha had planned to take the same flight. For almost twenty-four hours, her colleagues thought she had perished—until she turned on her phone and "returned from the underworld," which wasn't the first time.

They say that just before his death, the great Ukrainian writer and philosopher Hryhorii Skovoroda asked to have the following inscribed on his gravestone: "The world tried to catch me but failed." I remember this phrase whenever I think about my dear friend Alexandra Volgina. The Kremlin designed the cruel and pitiless idea of the "Russian world" in order to classify as non-human anyone who doesn't serve their purposes. And this Russian world keeps pursuing Sasha, someone always ready to help the most destitute, but for the last thirty-five years it has failed to catch her.

Black Avatars

From the first days of the war, the HIV treatment and prevention system in Ukraine—maybe it wasn't an ideal system, but it was certainly the best in Eastern Europe—collapsed.

Imagine a besieged city, such as Chernigov. Shelling, bombing, street fighting, people living in basements. If, for healthy people, a basement means no food or heat, for people living with HIV (or with diabetes, high blood pressure, or some forms of cancer) a basement means death. People who live with HIV shouldn't skip their meds, but for people undergoing substitution therapy, any break is a death sentence. This means that the entire system of drug distribution and substitution therapy must be adjusted under conditions of war when only emergency shipments are being sent to Ukraine. After crossing the border, Ukrainian civic organizations, such as 100% LIFE, will have to unload, distribute, and arrange humanitarian convoys.

But this is in theory. In practice things are more complicated. Support for HIV-positive individuals constitutes an enormous bureaucratic infrastructure formed over the course of decades. In times of peace, The Global Fund to Fight AIDS, the Ukrainian government, and the US President's Emergency Plan for AIDS Relief (PEPFAR) invested millions of dollars in Ukraine, but budgets had been calculated and approved, and the money allocated through proposals and grants before the war. Now everything had to be quickly changed and millions of additional dollars had to be invested. And you need to lobby for these emergency changes, explaining that war has its own rules. Approximately the same holds true for the Soros Fund, the Elton John Fund, and for the pharmaceutical giant GlaxoSmithKline—they allocate enormous amounts of money but aren't equipped to send help to locations under attack after receiving a frantic voice message. So, the needs of wartime have to be presented through applications, projects, and presentations.

Every day from dawn to dusk, Alexandra Volgina tries to convince partners and sponsors to adjust their approach. They need money not next year but now. Not only for medications but also for food. And they need to buy food not only for HIV-positive people but for everyone else who's sitting in that bomb shelter with them—it's impossible even to imagine how volunteers could enter those basements and begin feeding only those who have proof of their HIV-status without giving any food to the hungry old people and children sitting there next to them.

In addition to food, there is also a need for mattresses and blankets in the shelters (that's what Alexandra calls the refugee centers in the Western parts of Ukraine almost untouched by the war. Non-governmental organizations set up more than twenty such shelters in the first months of the war). And they need gas for buses. And there's another problem—the prisons, where there are many people not only with HIV but also with TB. One way or another, in an unbelievably short amount of time, Alexandra finds emergency money to help people in Ukraine living with HIV and everyone who lives with them—eight hundred thousand dollars. The machinery of aid has been set in motion. Through the efforts of a hundred people, medications are distributed, food and water are purchased, shelters are equipped and staffed with volunteers, and buses loaded with humanitarian aid begin to depart from Kyiv to, let's say, Chernihiv. And then the Russian army destroys the convoy with mortar fire. All the volunteers are killed. The black avatars Alexandra Volgina sees on social media when she wakes up in Amsterdam are for the fallen volunteers.

Inconvenient People

What would you have thought about these people six months before? They're vulnerable population groups? And now—they are heroes who sacrificed their lives to deliver medications, food, and water.

How do you see refugees in general? When we say the word "refugees," we most likely imagine a woman with a child, a helpless old woman, or a feeble old man. And you'd be right. Most refugees fit this description. And now imagine a refugee who's transgender.

A person arrives at a border checkpoint dressed in a woman's dress, with a woman's body underneath it, but this person's documents clearly state: Gender—Male. So, this person had changed their gender before the war but there was no time to change their papers. From a border control officer's point-of-view, this is a clear case of extreme cowardice—a man fleeing his homeland that is fighting for its survival disguised as a woman. But from the modern medical point of view, this person is a woman. And in accordance with stereotypical gender roles—this woman has two children under her care. It might be a bit too difficult for the border patrol officer to navigate modern gender theories but, in a few words, our future is standing there at this border checkpoint, dressed as a woman with a man's papers. It is a future in which the world is open to all people, the very same future the Russian armies are fighting against while pretending they're fighting fascism or the military encroachment of NATO.

Or imagine this: Market Square in Lviv. Two athletic young men in military uniforms walk by City Hall, and all the passersby greet them with applause, which has become the custom in Lviv since 2014. Is this male solidarity? Military comradeship? No! These are two lovers from different army divisions who were granted a three-day pass to visit their domestic partners before being shipped to the frontline. Russian propaganda can't even imagine something like that, and if they could, they would start screaming that there aren't only Nazis serving in the Ukrainian army but also gays who don't even try to hide their sexual orientation. The point is that the archaic Russian regime not only hates the future, it can't even imagine it. It can't imagine a world in which homosexual people have the same rights and obligations as heterosexual people.

The archaic part of Ukrainian society is also having a hard time. Olena Shevchenko, the director of the NGO Insight, which protects LGBTQ rights, and an activist in the Ukrainian feminist organization The March of Women, arrives in Lviv along with other refugees. And what does she do in Lviv? What do all activists do in Lviv? They load trucks with humanitarian aid, of course. There are only women in their organization, and in a single day several women load more than one ton of diapers and baby food until they're too tired to do any more. In one of Lviv's central streets, Olena lags behind her girlfriends and, as soon as she's alone, a man runs toward her, calls her by name, sprays her in the face with pepper spray, and runs away. Who is he? A Russian infiltrator trying to sabotage Ukrainian aid initiatives? No. As the police discover, he's a member of a right-wing radical nationalist organization—they used to threaten Olena only verbally, but now they got their chance to attack her physically.

To answer the question "Are there Nazis in Ukraine?" Yes, there are some, and this is who they are. The Nazis in Ukraine do exactly what the Russian government does: They persecute LGBT activists and obstruct the movement of humanitarian convoys. But we would be wrong to think that with his pepper spray, that bastard didn't think he was fighting evil and didn't have his own ideas of Ukraine's bright future. The question is: what kind of ideas. A country filled with docile women wearing traditional Ukrainian dresses? It's hard for him to believe that the road to Ukraine's future isn't paved with national costumes but with boxes of humanitarian aid.

Even for young Ukrainians, it's hard to imagine a future worth fighting for. Alexandra Volgina tells me about one of her charges—an HIV-positive refugee now in Amsterdam. The refugee asked her how to schedule an appointment with a doctor to get antiretroviral therapy while managing to keep her status a secret from her wonderful Dutch hosts who are letting her live in their house.

"Do you really think they shouldn't know anything?" Alexandra queries. "Tell them, and they'll help you find a doctor."

"No, if I tell them, they'll kick me out."

"Why would they kick you out?"

"Well . . . I have HIV!"

"Listen, here in the Netherlands, everyone understands that a person might have HIV."

"They understand it, and they aren't afraid?" "They understand it, and they aren't afraid." This is a key formula. The future worth fighting for is one in which people understand one another and aren't afraid of one another. The only problem is that it's very difficult for everyone to imagine such a future.

Quitting Cold Turkey

It's much easier to imagine the past. The past has already happened. Alexandra has seen it. In the past, it wasn't as if they intentionally tried to kill people; they just didn't take them into consideration.

When Russia annexed Crimea in 2014, Russian doctors faced a problem that no Russian politicians had anticipated—what to do with HIV-positive people in Crimea who are undergoing substitution therapy, that is, heroin addicts who are receiving methadone? In Russia, methadone programs are prohibited, substitution therapy is considered liberal bullshit, and doctors along with police are ordered to treat heroin, the cause of the addiction, the same as methadone, the treatment for that addiction. But there were people in Crimea who depended on methadone, and Russia took possession of them along with the other citizens of the peninsula.

Those who weren't able to escape Russia's grip and flee to Ukraine but instead asked doctors for help—dozens or even hundreds of people—were transported to Petersburg and checked into the toxicology wards of various clinics. To help them through their withdrawal, these patients were offered over-the-counter painkillers. Drug addicts call this torture "quitting cold turkey." Alexandra Volgina, for instance, quit "cold turkey," as if wanting to punish herself for having used drugs for so many years. That was her choice, conscious and complicated, but her drug use could be measured in years, not in decades. The Russian medical system forced Crimeans to withdraw "cold turkey" against their will. At international meetings and conferences, the doctors from Petersburg complained to Alexandra Volgina that those Crimean patients behaved terribly in their hospitals—they would swear, scream, try to escape, and even physically assault the staff.

"Do you realize that you were torturing them?" Alexandra responded, knowing all too well what she was talking about.

But the Russian doctors only shrugged their shoulders. They couldn't understand why it was wrong to torture people just because their native land had *de facto* stopped being Ukrainian territory and had become a part of Russia.

When the physical (but not psychological or social) withdrawal of Crimean patients was over, they were simply released onto the streets of Petersburg. And what did they do then? It's no mystery to any specialist—they went in search of drugs, which, of course, they found. But those were unknown drugs from unknown dealers in an unknown city—God only knows what they found. And within several days—as Alexandra testifies—all those people died from chemical poisoning and overdoses. All of them.

The past says: But they did it to themselves—no one forced them to do drugs again.

The future responds: But they had somehow lived before the annexation—they worked, had families, tried to treat their addiction, and they died when their treatment stopped.

And Alexandra Volgina asks: What's happening in Mariupol, in Kherson, in Berdiansk, and in the other cities now occupied by the Russian army? What's happening with the people that were undergoing substitution therapy? What's happening with people who are HIV-positive and haven't received their medications for three months?

The past says: Who cares? Let them die, it's all their fault.

The future says: First, they're people. Second, don't we treat people who have heart attacks because they've eaten too much red meat? Everyone has the right to medical treatment.

A Three-Day Vacation

Those are Alexandra's thoughts as she leaves for Kyiv to see her husband, a volunteer who received a three-day pass from the Military Forces of Ukraine to visit his wife before he's shipped to the frontline. Alexandra's passport was issued by Russia, the same country that ordered its soldiers to bomb Kyiv, to kill civilians in Bucha, and to destroy Mariupol.

She has no problems on her flight from Amsterdam to Warsaw, nor on the train from Warsaw to the border. When they reach the border, the customs officers and the train conductor are not sure Alexandra will be able to travel through Ukraine with her Russian passport, but they don't detain her. Her next train goes to Lviv, and Alexandra's already thinking she's made it across the border. Not so fast—in Lviv, Alexandra's taken off the train.

A very serious female customs officer interrogates her.

"To see your husband? Your husband's serving in the Ukrainian army? You left your children in Amsterdam? In what city is your husband serving?"

Alexandra names the city but in the Russian pronunciation.

"There's no such place in Ukraine."

Alexandra softens the final consonant, and that, it seems, softens the customs officer as well. What follows no longer resembles an attempt to ferret out a spy. With every minute that passes, it looks more like a conversation between two very tired women, one of them telling her life story to the other. How she was sick in Russia without any medical help, how she fought for her survival and, it seems, succeeded. How everything she'd created over the last ten years was destroyed. How she decided to have a child without a husband. How she moved to Kyiv and met a nice guy. How she had her second child. How her husband went to war because actually he was a really nice guy. How she was left in Amsterdam alone with two children. How she tried to help Ukraine and raised eight hundred thousand dollars.

"How much?" the customs officer asks again with a note of respect.

"Eight hundred thousand dollars, more like eight hundred fifty."

After that, Alexandra sits and listens as the female officer calls her boss in Kyiv, how in her Zapadensky dialect, which was difficult for Alexandra to understand, she explains that she has a good woman sitting in front of her—her husband's in the army, her children are in a foreign country, she raised eight hundred thousand . . . She's speaking in a kind voice, and the person on the other end of the line seems sympathetic too. But the female officer can't release Alexandra right away—she'll have to stay there over night until Kyiv sends permission for her to enter the country. And the officer calls the guards.

One of the guards is named Petro. He's a very tired-looking man with a machinegun. He picks up Alexandra's bag and takes her into the section of the railroad station that is closed to passengers during the war. There is no electricity, and they walk upstairs with a flashlight. Petro opens a door, leads Sasha inside, enters the room and locks it from the inside. There are only four chairs in the room and a tourist mat on the floor. The guard lets Sasha sleep on the chairs, makes himself comfortable on the mat and instantly falls asleep. Sasha writes to her husband on WhatsApp:

"I'm at the railroad station, locked in a room with a man with a machine gun ☺ And one day of your four-day-leave is already over ☹"

"☺," her husband answers. "And my boss shortened my break by one day."

It's cold in the room, not much above freezing. Sasha puts on all the clothes she's brought with her, lies down on the chairs that she's moved together, and tries to sleep.

She wakes up early from the cold and discomfort. She needs to use a bathroom, but the guard is still asleep. "Wake him up already!" her husband texts in WhatsApp. But Sasha feels sorry for this tired soldier who probably has a wife and children somewhere too and who probably hasn't slept in his own bed for three months already. "C'mon, wake him up!" her husband writes. And so Sasha, with a soft voice in Ukrainian, as if talking to a child, wakes up Petro—*Vibachte*.[6]

Petro wakes up and takes Sasha to the office. Her permission to enter the country is ready.

Kyiv looks strange to Sasha, even though she's lived there for many years. At first, she can't figure out what's so strange. Who cares about some cement barricades and a few anti-tank hedgehogs lining the sidewalks? That's not it—something else has changed. Then Sasha realizes that there are no children in the city. Kyiv, which has always been a child-friendly city and where the happy chatter of children was always louder than the traffic, is suddenly childless. Traffic is flowing through the streets, pedestrians are running errands, no one is paying any attention to the air-raid sirens, but there are no children anywhere. The future has been evacuated from the city. Here's another image of war for you—not a single child on the streets, not in the court yards, not on the playgrounds. And all the children's clothing stores are closed—there's no one to wear them.

---

[6] This means "excuse me" in Ukrainian.

For two days, Sasha and her husband live in their small apartment in the Pechersk neighborhood. After Sasha left for Amsterdam, they rented the place, but now their renters too have become refugees, and the apartment is empty. Just like in the first months of their romance, they live a completely carefree existence, and Sasha can't recall what they had ever fought about before the war. They did quarrel about things, didn't they? Didn't they argue? But what was it they argued about?

The two days quickly pass. On the third day, the lovers get in their parents' car to drive Sasha's husband to his military unit in the Chernihiv region. They drive through villages destroyed by the war. There are ruins on both sides of the road. Atop the ruins are white flags and signs that read CHILDREN written in white paint.

Sasha starts to cry for the first time since she began telling me her story: "What's happened to us, Valery? How could we bomb buildings where children were hiding? What's happened to us?"

In this case, "we" means Russians.

Chapter 9
The Hippocratic Oath

> "All civilians wishing to leave Mariupol for their safety may travel eastward along the Mariupol-Shirokova highway. This applies to residents of Kiev as well, who may leave the city in the direction of Vasilkovo. The Russian military will not present any obstacles to the departure of civilians."
> Official Representative of the Russian Ministry of Defense, Igor Konashenkov, March 2, 2022.

THE AZOV INSIGNIA

Dr. Vladimir Trunov is a pediatric surgeon who works in Moscow, in a hospital that belongs to the Federal Medical-Biological Agency (FMBA). In other words, it's a military hospital for children, or to be more precise—for the children of military personnel. As it so happens, the children of officers and soldiers get sick too, and in Russia there's a special healthcare system set up for them. Before the war, the only difference between pediatric hospitals for civilians and those for the military was their names. And Dr. Trunov never felt like a military man. But something changed after February 24—the doctors were offered business trips to the frontline. It wasn't mandatory, and they weren't forced—they were simply asked whether they wanted to go in Mariupol and help. It was difficult for Dr. Trunov to say "no" to such an offer. He's a doctor who took the Hippocratic Oath, and there are injured people in Mariupol. There's another reason that made it even more difficult to refuse—that feeling of living in historic times but staying on the sidelines when he could be a part of history in the making. In a word, the doctor agreed.

He was a little scared to go to the frontline. This fear came not from the possibility of being caught under fire, being injured, or even killed, but from the thought that his friends, Moscow doctors who were against the war, wouldn't understand his motives.

But I'm a doctor, I took the Oath, and I'm going to save people!

And so, our doctor decides to go to the war zone. In Moscow, he boards a train at the Kyrskiy railroad station and travels to Rostov. In addition to a small suitcase, the doctor brings boxes of medication—many boxes of antibiotics and antiseptics, bandages and suture materials.

In Rostov, the doctor loads his boxes on an FMBA truck and off they go to some place in the steppe. They cross the border of the Donetsk People's Republic—an entity recognized only by Russia—not through the usual border checkpoint where the buses with refugees go but through a military checkpoint, where armored vehicles from Russia move to the front of the line. The doctor doesn't remember the name of that border checkpoint or just doesn't want to tell me.

The Moscow doctors load their medications once again, this time on a military truck belonging to the Donetsk rebels, and continue driving.

Their driver is tired, unshaven, and angry, but he wants to talk, to tell the new people from Moscow how hard it's been for them—they've bombed us for eight years, wanted to enslave us, tried to force their language on us, but they picked the wrong people. Do you know what kind of people live in Donbas, Doctor, how stubborn we are, how resistant? We can't be made to do anything, do you understand? We've been here all alone, just us, but now we're with Russia. And thanks, Doctor, for coming here. Understand?

Over such conversations, they arrive at the resort in the village of Noviy Svet, and it feels like they've stepped back in time fifty years. Buildings that look like concrete boxes, without any hint of architectural design, a cement statue of a young pioneer who used to be happy but is now without an arm, and a fountain without water. This is where they'll be living. And they'll be working in the village of Mangush on the outskirts of Mariupol, in the district hospital where the only medical equipment is an X-ray machine. Considering that almost all their patients are refugees and almost all of them have mine-blast injuries, an X-ray is the only diagnostic tool they'll need. At this moment, our doctor draws his first conclusion: In war, medicine gets simplified and becomes battle-field medicine. In times of war, medicine has little to do with rare or chronic diseases—it treats only injuries. And it's not that difficult to treat the injured considering that in many cases the doctor administers only emergency first aid and sends more serious cases to Donetsk.

There are many injured, and they arrive one after the other. An eight-hour shift is easily stretches into a ten- or twelve-hour shift. It's good they don't have any free time. What would you do here with free time? So, the doctor operates, applies splints to broken limbs, stitches wounds, and injects antibiotics. Most wounds are old and infected—phlegmon, pseudomonas sepsis, sometimes even gangrene. People are saying that Ukrainian soldiers didn't allow them to leave the city, even prohibited them from leaving their shelters, and sometimes going so far as to weld the doors of their apartment buildings and basements shut with blowtorches.

"But why was it possible to leave only after your injury got infected?"

"The Russians came and evacuated us."

What is the doctor to think? He believes them. Why would people lie, especially to the doctor who is stitching up their wounds or setting their broken bones?

Most wounds are from shards of shrapnel, but some are from sniper bullets. People say that the Ukrainian snipers, especially the snipers from the Azov Battalion, considered any civilian who was running down the street as a legitimate target and would shoot them.

There's a girl with complex, splintered fractures in both legs. The girl's mom is saying:

"She was just running across the street. What kind of monster must you be to shoot a child? And it's not like we didn't need to go outside. We were running to get some water from a spring—there was no water in the basement."

The doctor has a hard time believing this. It's hard to comprehend why a Ukrainian sniper would suddenly shoot at his compatriots, peaceful civilians, especially children. Why?

But then a woman arrives with a shoulder injury. Once in her shoulder, the bullet changed direction and entered her neck. This woman says that she just wanted to adjust a blanket over her window, so she approached the window, stepped onto the windowsill, and then the shot hit her. The doctor operates on the woman and extracts the bullet. The bullet is American, from an American sniper rifle. The doctor can't really see the difference between American and Russian bullets, but local officers insist the bullet is American. They even show him a cartridge from a Russian sniper rifle: *Look Doctor, our bullets are different. We're telling you, they're monsters—they're animals, not people.*

The injured keep arriving. One of them says he saw it with his own eyes how a soldier wearing the Azov Battalion insignia pulled out his gun on a street in Mariupol and for no reason whatsoever shot an elderly man who was hobbling to the spring to get some water. Another says he saw soldiers of the Azov Battalion pillaging stores. A third recounts how he and his pregnant wife were stopped at a Ukrainian checkpoint. First, the soldier threatened to conscript him immediately into the army, but then, after he and his wife begged the soldier to spare the husband of a pregnant woman, the soldier took all their money and all the rings from the woman's fingers and let them pass. After that he fired at the back of their car anyway.

This is how they tell their stories, and after listening to dozens of stories about the soldiers of the Azov Battalion, the doctor draws his second conclusion: For some reason, Ukrainian soldiers don't consider people from the Donetsk and Luhansk regions as their compatriots but see them instead as some kind of second-class temporary residents of Eastern Ukraine. It's impossible for the doctor to come up with another conclusion from all the stories he's heard about soldiers wearing the Azov Battalion insignia. It's very difficult to find any other explanation.

"But where do they wear those insignias?" I ask the doctor.
"What?"
"Where is the insignia worn? On the right shoulder? On the left? On the chest?"
"I don't know," Doctor answers. "I've never seen any."

At this point you might ask how it happened that the doctor had never seen any prisoners even though he'd been working in the vicinity of the frontline. Was it because medical help wasn't extended to prisoners? Or was it because they weren't taking any prisoners?

But even a question about the insignia was quite enough. Several times, when refugees on the Russian side were telling me about the crimes committed by the soldiers of the Azov Battalion, I'd ask them about the insignia: *Where exactly was it displayed?* And every time this question would throw my interlocuter into the deepest confusion. *Really, where was it? On the chest, on the left shoulder, on the right?*

I'm not trying to say that the soldiers of the Azov Battalion weren't capable of cruelty. Of course, they were. Everybody acts cruelly during war. I suppose the refugees on the Russian side repeat the phrase "A soldier with the Azov Battalion insignia injured me" as a protective prayer. They are expected to complain about the cruelty of the Ukrainian Nazis, and so they complain about soldiers with the Azov insignia.

I shared this thought with the doctor, but he didn't agree with me. No, he saw the injured with his own eyes, he operated on them with his own hands. In the ambulance, he accompanied five seriously wounded individuals to Donetsk. The road was destroyed, the bridge was bombed out, and so they had to take a detour through small towns and villages. He saw a bus with refugees that had pulled over to the side of the road and was blown up by a mine.

Donetsk impressed him. The city was standing proud—there were flowers everywhere, cafés and theaters were operating. The people were showing unprecedented courage. The people are determined to destroy the enemy, but the enemy is strong, well-equipped, and trained by NATO instructors.

"Doctor, are you planning to come back?" I ask.

"Yes," the doctor answers. "I'll come back. We have to help."

A DOCTOR FROM AMERICA

Dr. Evgeny Pinelis had the same idea—he, too, believes it's necessary to help. He's a critical care doctor from New York City. It's a custom among doctors. Instead of going to Cancun, it's normal for a doctor to go somewhere to volunteer—to a war zone or to the site of an epidemic. One of his colleagues, for instance, went to Syria. Another colleague—to Africa, to treat an outbreak of Ebola. It's now considered normal for an American doctor of Russian descent to write to the Global Disaster Relief Team, the organization of Russian-speaking doctor-volunteers that was created in response to the Russian invasion of Ukraine. A doctor asks whether help is needed, and if so, what kind of help and where.

Dr. Pinelis, too, brings boxes of medication. First, he travels by plane from New York, then through Vienna and Warsaw to

Rzeszów, and after that by train to Przemyśl. But this doctor has brought different drugs: They aren't antibiotics or bandage and suture materials, they're mostly headache pills, stomachache remedies, and most importantly—Plan B, the morning-after pill that women should take within forty-eight hours after being raped so as to avoid getting pregnant, as well as abortion pills.

In Poland, there's a real need for these drugs. The Polish people accept the Ukrainians with open arms as close friends and relatives. But abortion is prohibited in Poland, even chemical abortions, even out of medical necessity, even in cases of rape. In Western Ukraine, which is traditionally Catholic, abortions aren't easy to get either.

Dr. Pinelis won't meet any victims of rape; volunteers will take all the drugs to Ukraine. But while loading his boxes of drugs in Rzeszów, he can't help thinking: "If I was asked to bring this many doses of Plan B, and I'm not the only one bringing them—all the volunteer doctors are doing the same—then how many women have been raped during this war?"

Twelve American doctors live in Przemyśl in a spacious four-bedroom country house. It's three people per room, but with shifts lasting from ten to twelve hours, they come home only to sleep. Their job is mostly that of a paramedic. There are very few injured, sometimes cases of shellshock and concussions from explosions. Most of the injured are treated in Ukraine, in Zaporizhzhia, Kyiv, or Lviv. Except for the cases of post-traumatic stress disorder—people with a frozen gaze and zombie-like voice—most of the cases Dr. Pinelis has to deal bear witness not so much to the horrors of the war but to the horrors of the pre-war Ukrainian health care system.

As a rule, people bring huge bags of drugs, sometimes instead of warm clothes. And in most cases, people don't even need those drugs, and they have no idea about what drugs might actually help. And they're very surprised when everyone who comes to see Dr. Pinelis gets a prescription for vitamin D.

There's a man with legs covered in diabetic ulcers, almost gangrenous. He doesn't know anything about diabetes and has never monitored his sugar level. He needs to be thoroughly examined in a clinic, for instance, in Warsaw. And there's a woman with severe bradycardia—her heart beats no more than fifty times a minute.

"Are you taking any blood pressure medication?" the doctor asks.

"Yes, I am."

"What medications?"

"A round white pill and a red oval one."

The doctor quietly curses the hack who prescribed these to the poor woman and cancels both prescriptions—for the round one and the oval one. He prescribes the minimal dose of beta blockers instead, and in two days, he sees the woman walking through the refugee camp in noticeably improved condition.

Another woman has the opposite problem—she's taking antihypertension drugs only when she feels pain at the back of her head, in other words, when her blood pressure rises. The doctor explains to her that, to treat high blood pressure, she needs to take her medication regularly—it's very simple, every third-year medical student knows that. And the doctor thinks: Where are the people who are seriously ill? It can be assumed that HIV-positive people are concealing their status out of fear. But where are the oncology patients? The doctor hasn't seen any.

There's a kid with a toothache. They'll have to find him a dentist in Przemyśl or in Rzeszów ASAP. The volunteers there will help.

There's also a kid with a cold. He got sick back in the bomb shelter and, since then, his mother has been feeding him antibiotics, which she gets by hook or by crook, even bartering her earrings. The doctor spares no time or effort convincing the mother that she must stop the antibiotics.

Here's a case of upset stomach, another upset stomach, and

more such cases. Diarrhea, diarrhea, and diarrhea again. The doctor thinks: *If there are so many people with stomach viruses in winter, what will happen in the summer? It's likely there will be an outbreak of cholera in Mariupol, which will spread to other sea-side towns.*

And finally, there's a man with a sharp pain in his chest. How can we help him? Have him lie down, give him some nitroglycerin, and when the pain subsides, send him to get a cardiogram in the Israeli medical tent. The American medical tent in Przemyśl doesn't have a cardiograph machine.

The job is simple, but there's a lot to do. You might see thirty patients in a single shift, sometimes forty, or even fifty. When his shift ends, the doctor leaves the tiny room in the former mall that was assigned to him as an office, inhales some relatively fresh air, and hears a woman's sobbing.

"Help me, help me . . . "

"What's wrong? Are you hurt? Where's the pain?"

The woman keeps crying, unable to explain what's wrong. Only several minutes later is the doctor able to make out through her sobbing that she lost her backpack—the backpack with all her papers, money, and a photo from home.

"Please, stop crying, let's go look for your backpack."

And off they go, walking past empty display windows where mannequins once modelled the latest fashion and now transport volunteers put refugees on the buses. They walk through the shopping area where booths with perfumes and costume jewelry once stood and now soldiers set up beds for the night.

"Here's your backpack!" the doctor exclaims after noticing a bag lying in a corner.

"No, it's not mine. Mine was red," the woman answers and starts crying again. "All my papers, money, and the special photo."

Now they're looking not only for the woman's lost backpack but also for the owner of the backpack found by the doctor.

They keep wandering through the shopping mall until, at some point, the woman disappears. She probably lost all hope of recovering her valuables. And when the doctor finally finds the red backpack, there's no one to return it to. So, the doctor keeps walking through the shopping mall now with two backpacks, looking for their owners. Finally, he finds the woman, witnesses her joy but can't help thinking: *What am I doing here? Is it right that a highly qualified ER doctor is treating scratches and looking for lost backpacks? Where are the real patients? They must be somewhere. Is anyone actually treating them?*

This is what the doctor thinks, and this is how emotional exhaustion sets in. The exhaustion comes according to schedule—on about the sixth day, when Dr. Pinelis's trip is almost over. The doctor goes back to New York, returns to work, and realizes how lucky he is to work in the hospital's ER, with its fast pace and tight schedule, instead of the total chaos of the refugee camp.

Two Oksanas

Oksana B. is running down the stairs from the fifteenth floor with a three-month-old infant in her arms. Her husband's running behind her with a stroller and a bag they quickly packed with the baby's food and clothes. Baby food is of the utmost importance as Oksana doesn't have any breast milk. She has breast cancer. Before the war, in Kyiv she underwent a mastectomy and five courses of chemotherapy. The sixth course was scheduled for the beginning of March, but the war began. They live in Brovary, a small town near Kyiv, and their multi-storey apartment building is right across from the military base where—just as we're speaking—missiles begin to land. So, Oksana and her husband don't wait, they don't hesitate for a moment—they flee on the morning of February 24.

Oksana M., too, has breast cancer, but she lives in Mariupol. She, too, has undergone a mastectomy and now needs targeted drugs—a state-of-the-art treatment that detects and destroys malignant cells (blocking or turning off the signals that make cancer cells grow, or signaling the cancer cells to attack themselves). But the war has begun and there are no more drugs. Oksana isn't fleeing because the local authorities have announced that the roads are closed and that no one should leave. Mariupol is protected by the most combat-ready division of the Ukrainian army, so there isn't any danger. Oksana and her husband are hiding in the basement of the Priazovskiy State Technical University along with two hundred other civilians. They only had time to buy some potatoes, apples, and *adjika*, a local spice, and this constitutes their contribution to the collective food supply. The civilians get organized—they take turns cooking food for the whole group and cleaning up. When it's Oksana's turn to cook, she goes outside, starts the fire, but at that very moment, Russian planes approach, and the bombing begins. She falls face down on the ground. From the force of the explosions, the cooking pot tips over and the soup mixes with the mud.

Dr. Pinelis wondered where the seriously ill patients were and who was helping them. Here they are! And no one is helping them; they are not being treated for their life-threatening diseases. They're busy just staying alive. They're not thinking about how not to die in a month—they're thinking about how not to die today.

Oksana B., along with her husband and baby, get into their car and travel to the Zhitomir region where her mother lives. But there's bombing there too, and in any case, there has never been an oncologist in that region. So, they take her mother along with them and drive on, to Lviv. Oksana's next course of chemotherapy is long overdue. Only in Lviv is Oksana able to find an oncologist. She gets one IV treatment, and then they tell her that there are no more medications and that she should go to the West. From the beginning of the war, there have been no oncological drugs in Ukraine, and all oncological surgeries have been postponed for an unknown period. The people who will die as a result—will they be counted among the military losses?

In Mariupol, Oksana M. and her husband leave the basement of the university and go to a real bomb shelter, where the walls are covered in Soviet era posters explaining how one should lie on the floor in case of a nuclear explosion. In this bomb shelter, no one shares their food anymore. There is almost no food. Oksana has only a small box with some candies and cookies. It was given to Oksana by a girl whose older brother tried to evacuate her from the city on his own. No one knows if he succeeded or not.

For breakfast, Oksana has a piece of candy and a cookie along with some of the remaining *adjika*. There is no lunch. For dinner, it's again a piece of candy and a cookie with a little *adjika*. There is no water. In the first days of the war, Ukrainian soldiers brought water. They don't anymore. Oksana's husband goes out under the shelling to get some water from the spring. During one of these expeditions, he finds two jars of sauerkraut in a bombed out military base. He's happy to bring them to his wife. I wonder if that's considered looting. So now there's a candy, a cookie, *adjika*, sauerkraut, and a glass of water for breakfast. It doesn't even occur to anyone to think about the targeted drugs Oksana needs to begin taking after her surgery.

With the help of Rubikus volunteers, Oksana B. crosses the border and travels to Stuttgart, Germany. They're already waiting for her. A nice elderly couple allows them to stay in their apartment with the baby as long as necessary. In a local clinic, Oksana already has an appointment with an oncologist. How exactly the volunteers managed to find her this host family and the doctor, Oksana doesn't really know.

The clinic shocks Oksana. Apparently, it's no longer necessary to look for a vein on her wrist or the inside of her elbow that's not too bruised from previous injections. Instead, they insert a catheter into Oksana's subclavian vein—and that's it, there's no need for any injections.

Apparently, in Germany if the chemo is scheduled at nine o'clock in the morning, it will begin at nine in the morning. In Ukraine, it was different. If the procedure is scheduled in the morning, you're lucky if you receive it in the evening, after hours of waiting in line and several quarrels with the staff.

It turns out, it's possible to receive chemotherapy as an outpatient. There's no need to stay in the hospital. There's even no need to lie down—you can sit and watch TV while receiving your IV.

It turns out, in Germany, when patients undergo chemotherapy, they get special cooling down gloves for the hands and special cooling down socks to protect their nails from the highly toxic drugs. No one has even heard about this in Ukraine.

When the war is over, when Oksana B. and other refugees with cancer return home, they'll bring back to Ukraine these advances in medical care. In a strange way, this humanitarian crisis may bring about a health care revolution in Ukraine—as patients return and demand change.

Oksana M., for instance, will talk about the ambulances when she returns home. Oksana ended up in the Austrian city of Krems an der Donau by chance—she got a piece of advice from a former colleague, a famous fortune teller in Mariupol, and the choirmaster at the music school where Oksana used to work as the concertmaster. This fortune teller spread out her cards, called Oksana, and informed her in an authoritative voice: *You should go to Austria, the cards are telling me—Austria.* When she arrived in Krems, Oksana had no idea how to book a doctor's appointment and asked her volunteer from Rubikus for help. That volunteer simply called the emergency number and an ambulance came and took Oksana to the hospital. The next day she was receiving, entirely for free, the targeted therapy she couldn't have dreamed about in that Mariupol basement.

A Surgeon's Tools

Mikhail Kaabak is a professor and a transplant surgeon well-known not only in Moscow, not only in Russia, but throughout world—he's prominent in the field of advanced medical technologies. The professor is invited to Mariupol by another famous doctor, Badma Bashankayev, who was recently elected to the Russian State Duma from the United Russia Party and is an avid supporter of the Russian invasion of Ukraine, but at the same time, he's a doctor, a humanitarian. How all this can coexist in one person is a mystery to me.

In Donetsk and Mariupol, Professor Kaabak has been tasked with helping to organize the local health care system—any, even the most primitive, as there is currently none.

In Donetsk, the professor is assigned to the Children's Hospital of the Donetsk People's Republic. It's a rather good hospital, with relatively decent equipment. The doctors at this hospital are generally well trained but, to be honest, over the last eight years of military conflict, these doctors have significantly fallen behind as they haven't been able to read any scientific journals or attend any conferences. In this hospital, all the storage rooms are overflowing with diapers, toys, and baby food. But there are no sutures, no surgical thread. And there are no instruments for conducting laparoscopy surgery.

In that hospital, the professor sees a two-year-old girl with a severe genetic malformation of the intestines. It's impossible to help her in Donetsk, so the famous Moscow professor uses his credentials to have the girl transferred to the Russian capital on a military helicopter. The girl is saved, but it's impossible to send everybody who needs complex surgery to Moscow by military helicopter.

There are about twenty injured children among the patients the professor is examining. Most of the injuries are on their backs, and this makes a strong impression on the professor. It's hard for him to imagine a soldier who would shoot a child in the back. Of course, everyone is saying that those were soldiers from the Azov Battalion. And the professor starts to believe it.

On the second or third day, the professor is examining a boy of about one year old (judging from his four teeth) named Seryozha. The toddler's well-fed and well taken care of—judging by his appearance, he was loved by his parents. At the beginning of the war, this boy was left at the hospital's door with a note saying: *We're going to fight for Ukraine. Please, take care of Seryozha.* And there were no other papers. The boy can already say a few words—mama, papa, but there is no mama or papa there for him. The professor begins to contemplate the boy's future after the war but can't come up with any reasonable scenario. He then gets distracted by other less difficult tasks and stops thinking about the boy's future.

There are water outages in the hospital. Running out of water is a common thing in Donetsk, and water outages are a regular occurrence. The Ministry of Health doesn't get any water at all.

On the fourth day, the delegation of Moscow doctors proceeds to Mariupol. In Professor Kaabak's words, about half the city is destroyed. There are no hospitals, and the doctors operate, not with scalpels, but mostly with hammers and power drills. With his own hands, the world-famous surgeon repurposes places that are unsuitable for practicing medicine—post offices, schools, and gyms—into outpatient care clinics and paramedic stations. He carries in generators so the doctors have light; he repairs pipes so the clinics have water; and he boards up windows destroyed by shelling.

When the first paramedic stations are almost ready, Professor Kaabak begins looking for doctors. There are doctors in Mariupol who are living amid the ruins and want to get back to work. But the administrative protocols of the occupiers must be followed: Doctors have to be legally registered and sign an official contract with the Ministry of Health of the Republic of Donetsk.

To legally register doctors, first, you have to take them to Donetsk and make sure they get certified. To get from Mariupol to Donetsk, however, one must pass through a filtration point. Remember Denys D.'s story? You have to strip to your underwear, then they check your tattoos and scars, search through your cellphone, and subject you to a thorough interrogation— *Who do you know in Azov? Who do you know in the army? Who do you know in the police? Have you ever served in either? Why not?* If Denys D. had to wait at the filtration point for several hours, the wait now, after the Russian army's capture of Mariupol, is no less than two weeks. And filtration is unavoidable. Professor Kaabak, along with the chief medical doctor of the Donetsk hospital and the Donetsk Deputy Minister of Health, manage to reach an agreement with the military on only one thing—allowing the doctors to go through the filtration point without waiting in line and making sure the entire process takes no more than two hours.

In the whirlwind of all these undertakings, Professor Kaabak notices that he is gradually beginning to feel sympathy for the people he's working with—not only with the Donetsk doctors, but also with the Donetsk military men and the military men from the Russian occupation army. The professor is shocked by their extreme bitterness, but rather than dwell on that, he's inclined to acknowledge the reasons behind it, and even accept that they might be right in some cases. They tell the professor stories about the referendum that took place in Mariupol and how the citizens voted to become part of Russia. This is precisely why the soldiers from the Azov Battalion consider them traitors, temporary residents, and why they torture, rampage, and pillage. Time after time, the professor hears the story of how soldiers from the Azov Battalion looted and pillaged, killing civilians, shooting rounds from tanks through the windows of residential buildings. And then there are those children with bullets in their backs—who complete the picture.

"You know," the professor says, "the Russian propaganda isn't all lies. The information on Russian TV is about ninety percent correct. For the most part, you have to admit the military of the Donetsk Republic is not always wrong. There's just one thing . . . the extreme bitterness . . . "

"Professor," I ask, "what do you mean by 'extreme bitterness?'"

"They don't take prisoners," Prof. Kaabak answers. "Only the Russian army takes prisoners in this war. The Donetsk army kills everyone."

What Refugees See

I can believe there's been cruelty on both sides of the conflict. I've been in four wars, and it seems to me that sooner or later all the participants become pitiless and bitter. It's much more difficult for me to believe the evidence of this cruelty. Because, do you know what the civilians and refugees see during the war? They see nothing.

Denys D., as you may remember, was an engineer at the Mariupol railroad car assembly plant. Even before the war, he hadn't paid much attention to political news. *The referendum? Well, yeah, there was some kind of referendum in 2014, I think. They gave us a few sheets of paper that didn't look like official documents—they didn't even have seals. Someone was voting for something. One person could vote several times—no one was checking.* It never occurred to Denys or to anyone he knew in Mariupol to participate in that referendum.

Ukrainian nationalists? Pro-Russian traitors? Denys says there wasn't anything like that in their city. *Well, yes, of course, there were people who spoke Russian and thought it would be better to become part of Russia. There were people who spoke Ukrainian and dreamed about Ukraine someday joining the European Union. But they all lived together.* Denys speaks fluently in both languages. *Sure, people would get into arguments, but those disagreements never led to anything, not even fist fights*—Denys doesn't remember any.

Right before the war, however, Denys built a house for his family. On February 24, when the first shots were fired, Denys didn't worry too much—shelling had happened before but rarely, far away and on a small scale. This time it was getting heavier and heavier, moving closer to the houses, without any sign of a lull.

Denys has a wife and two children. Why didn't they leave right away? Because in the city's public chatrooms people kept saying there was no reason to flee, that Mariupol was protected by very capable military divisions. But on the second day of the war, the lights went out. On the third day, they lost telephone communication. Until their evacuation at the end of March, Denys could access almost no information about what was happening on the frontlines, he didn't know anything about the humanitarian corridors for refugees, and he didn't know if his friends and relatives were even alive.

The bombing was coming closer every day. Denys and his family moved into his sister's house, which was closer to the city center. Her house had a basement, and she still had electricity, heat, and gas, which would last for only two more days. To get online, Denys would climb onto the roof, hoping to get a signal. But the connection was unreliable—it worked for one or two minutes, and then it was totally unstable again.

There was no longer any water. It's good they had the sense to fill up the bathtub. They tried to stock up on food, candles, matches, and warm clothes. Denys decides to go back to his house to get some food and clothes, but as soon as he reaches his house, war planes appear and start bombing. A missile hits their neighbor's house. The explosion knocks Denys to the ground, and pieces of wood and brick fall on top of him. Denys lies motionless on his stomach for some time, and when the shelling begins to subside, he jumps up and starts running. He doesn't remember how long he ran. He didn't see who was shooting. Only when he's escaped the gunfire does Denys realize that he left his pushcart near his house. This is a big loss. These days, it's hard to live in Mariupol without a pushcart. Their water supply was almost gone, and the spring was about ten kilometers away. How much water can you bring back in your hands? And they needed water for two families—his own and his sister's, for a total of seven people.

The next day Denys goes back to his house and manages to get his car from the garage. But you can't go to the spring by car. There was very little gas left, and the only source of gas was the looters who drain it from bombed-out cars and sell it for a thousand hryvnias per liter, which is twenty times higher than the pre-war price.

There is no communication, no food, and the temperature outside is well below freezing. It's below freezing inside the house too. Denys decides to go to his house one more time—there's some canned food left, but he runs into his neighbor and learns that his house doesn't exist anymore. It's been destroyed by bombs.

The two families move into Denys's mother's house, which has a furnace. And she has a pushcart. Denys and his brother-in-law take turns getting water. It's a long way. All the streets are covered with chunks of brick and shards of glass. There are corpses lying on the streets. If people find a body of a relative or an acquaintance, they bury them in their vegetable garden or in the city park. No one buries strangers; their corpses lie on the streets.

Has Denys seen any looting? Yes, he has, when they were looting the stores. But the looters weren't soldiers from the Azov Battalion, and they weren't Russian military men either. They were simple people, civilians, who were looting the stores. They were taking everything, from food to pieces of construction Styrofoam and rolls of linoleum. Denys realizes that Styrofoam and linoleum could be very useful for winterizing basements.

Has Denys seen any military men? Yes, he has, twice. Once he saw two Ukrainian soldiers at the spring. The soldiers offered Denys some cigarettes. Denys doesn't smoke but he took the cigarettes anyway. He doesn't remember any insignias or other distinguishing regalia.

The second time was when Denys was returning from the spring and got caught under shelling. He leaves his pushcart on the road, hides in a ditch, and sees a soldier crossing the street some distance away. Denys doesn't even know if the soldier was Russian or Ukrainian. And that's it. For a whole month and over many trips to the spring, he hasn't run into a single soldier—only missiles and bullets flying from different directions. This is why it's so hard for me to believe the refugees' stories about how they not only run into soldiers but also manage to identify their insignias.

Their food is almost gone. Denys climbs a tower carrying high-voltage power lines and finally gets a strong signal. He logs into his social networks to learn something about how people are managing to evacuate from Mariupol. They say it's better to leave in a column of cars—civilian columns are rarely shelled.

Denys's neighbors form a column of twenty-two cars. His parents refuse to go, saying they've lived here their entire life and they might as well die here too. Denys leaves them almost all their food although he realizes it won't last even a month.

The column leaves at dawn. They secure their car windows with suitcases. They put the children between the suitcases and tell them to bend down and cover themselves with a pile of blankets. With white paint, they write "Children" on the car doors and set off. They agree that no one stops—*You can't stop no matter what happens. Follow the first car and that's it. If you get a flat tire, keep moving. If a missile hits the first car, just drive around it and keep moving.*

The column is making its way through the city center when fighting suddenly breaks out around them. The shots seem to be coming from tanks—the sound is that loud. Denys thinks the tanks are firing at one another, and their column just happened to land in the middle of it.

Everything around them is black with smoke. Denys can see only the bumper of the big van in front of him. The road is littered with destroyed cars, bricks, and fallen electrical wires. Denys gets a flat—on all four tires—but he keeps driving.

One missile falls right in front of the big van Denys is following. The adults in the front seats have probably been killed or injured. The big van stops, its doors fly open, and kids jump out of the car and run away. People then start jumping out of their cars to catch those kids. They pull them, kicking and screaming, into their cars and keep driving. There are explosions all around them, and it's as dark as night. Denys can't hear what his wife is screaming.

"What?"

Another explosion!

"The boy ran away!"

"What?"

More explosions!

"The boy is hiding near the entrance."

"What?"

Still more explosions!

Denys says it might be that one of the children from the big van, a five-year-old boy, was left behind. He probably ran away and was hiding in one of the buildings along the road. It all happened in the middle of a battle, and so they couldn't search for the boy. No one knows where that little boy is now.

About an hour later, twenty of the original twenty-two cars, all with flat tires, reach the Ukrainian checkpoint where soldiers let the column pass without any complications. Thirty minutes later, they approach the Russian checkpoint. After that—well, you know the story: search, small bribes, petty stealing.

But the fact is, these are the first soldiers Denys has come across. In Mariupol itself, I repeat, Denys didn't see any soldiers. He saw only planes in the sky, explosions around him, looting, injuries, hunger, thirst, and death. Why? Because civilians and refugees don't see the war that surrounds them. Just like prey in the belly of a predator, they can't see what exactly swallowed them.

Chapter 10
A Digitized War

"The Spring recruitment drive is coming to an end. More than eighty-nine thousand conscripts have arrived at their assigned units. Conscription events are being carried out by military commissariats as scheduled. Military platoons are being assembled in a timely manner, and there have been no disruptions in the supply of new recruits. The mission to enlist civilians has been fully accomplished. Upon completing their term of service, the conscripts return to their places of residence. Conscripted military personnel will not be sent to the zone of the special military operation." Russian Minister of Defense, Army General Sergey Shougu, July 5, 2022.

MILLIONS OF TESTIMONIES

It was said that the 1990 Gulf War was broadcast live on CNN. About the 2022 Ukrainian war, one could say that every minute has been broadcast on social media.

This war is digitized, every single episode captured on digital media. No wonder the Russian military searches refugees' phones so thoroughly at the filtration checkpoints. But, no matter how hard they try to prevent it, information finds its way out. Even from the occupied territories, even from under bombardment, even from the very hell of combat, information is leaking out and social media users are posting their stories, photos, and videos. Not to mention the refugees themselves—there are millions of testimonies on the Internet.

Here's a photo of food boiling in a big camp pot on the streets of Bucha. Here's a photo of an intersection where Russian soldiers are executing a civilian bicyclist. Here's another of an infant born in a basement in Mariupol. Here's a photo of the people in that basement taking care of a newborn—coddling it, feeding it, and changing its diapers. Here's a photo of an eighteen-year-old soldier lying in a hospital bed. He lost his leg in a bomb explosion. He could go to America where they'll correctly form the stump and design a well-fitted prosthetic—but his documents were lost in combat, and the commanders don't have the time to request new documents for the injured.

This book could have been a hundred, even a thousand times longer. All I would have had to do was browse through social media, write to people who had posted their testimonies, and ask for more details, prodding their memories, and then edit the stories of those who wanted to talk. And I'd have had to offer my apologies to those who didn't want to relive their painful memories and to those who were disgusted at the very idea of talking to a Russian journalist and using the Russian language.

There are millions of witnesses. Some are very eager to share their experiences, while others refuse to talk; even so—there are millions who want to give their testimony. It is very likely that, sooner or later, a witness will be found for every incident of this war, even the most covert; indirect evidence will be compared by experts, and we'll know the truth—the truth about everything.

The social networks are fast; information there travels faster than a rocket. Take Anton Motolko, a host on the TV channel *Belarusian Gayun*, who posts that just a second ago a rocket was launched from Belarusian territory in the direction of Ukraine. And while this rocket was still in the air, Ukrainian forces had enough time to read Motolko's message, activate their air defense missiles, and shoot down the rocket.

Gayun, by the way, is a character from Belarusian fairytales, a know-it-all wood-sprite who collects information from all the birds and animals in the forest. The authorities in Minsk have labelled *Belarusian Gayun* an extremist channel and try to close it down, but in vain—can you really control all the birds and animals in the forest? Or all the bloggers on the Internet?

By itself, a chance photo or video can't provide a true picture of the war. But if you match it with other photos, videos, radio intercepts, and phone tracking data, then the fog of war begins to dissipate and secret military information becomes not just available, it becomes available for the entire world to see.

Who, for example, was shelling Donetsk? It's logical to conclude that it was the Ukrainians because the Russian troops and separatists were occupying the city. And this is what is reported on Russian TV: *Ukraine is shelling civilians in Donetsk.* But the videos of this shelling raise doubts—too little time passed between "minus" and "plus." In the language of military specialists, a "minus" is the bang you hear when a missile is fired, and a "plus" is the explosion heard when the missile hits its target. The Conflict Intelligence Team, a group of young people who gather and analyze war crime testimony, painstakingly locate the site where the video was taken; based on the buildings visible in the frame, they determine the exact location in Donetsk where the video was recorded. Then it becomes clear that there was not enough time between the minus and the plus. The nearest Ukrainian troops were nine kilometers away, which means a Ukrainian missile would have been in the air several seconds longer. This at least casts some doubt on the statement that it was the Ukrainians who fired the missile. Now, we can entertain the notion that the separatists themselves were shelling their own city in order to show shards of NATO missiles of unknown origin on TV and to proclaim that NATO weaponry is being used against civilians.

Or take the opposite situation, in Mariupol. Who shelled the Vostochny district? Russian TV insists that the Ukrainians were firing on their own civilians, which demonstrates their brutality and savagery. But there are plenty of photos and videos of the shell crates posted on social media. These photos allow us to do "crate-tometry analysis" and determine exactly what kind of missile was fired and from which side. And what do we learn? That there were no Ukrainian troops in the location where this missile was launched, but the Russian army was there. And so, it's no surprise that criminal charges have been filed in Russia against Ruslan Leviev, the leader of the Conflict Intelligence Team.

Ruslan says that their investigative work is a creative process. It's not enough to apply a dozen or so established research strategies—you need to be constantly coming up with new tactics and approaches.

Until just recently, Instagram, for instance, allowed the detection of the precise location of a user. And countless times, Ruslan's team was able to calculate the location of soldiers from the pictures they posted. After that, not only was Instagram banned in Russia, but Instagram itself turned off its location feature. "It's no problem," Ruslan says. "We'll come up with other detection methods."

Until the end of March, it was possible to track the movement of train cars on the official site of the Russian Railroad—all you had to know was the train car's number, which is written in big digits on the car itself, and on that site, which is completely open to the public, you can find out exactly where this car was loaded with military vehicles, where the car was heading, and when it arrived and was unloaded. Only at the end of March, after one month of war, did it occur to the Russian special forces to classify such information.

Now the Conflict Intelligence Team works mainly on summarizing military information, on tracing troops to see which military division bombed a particular city or to determine whether it's true that a Russian general pronounced dead by the Ukrainian army is indeed dead. But sooner or later, all the details of this humanitarian catastrophe will come to light and be investigated.

Remember that boy who ran away from the bombed car and hid somewhere in the middle of a tank battle in Mariupol? It's possible to find that boy if he's still alive. Ruslan Leviev says that if the boy's relatives—grandmothers, grandfathers, someone who recognizes the boy—contact him, then his team could scan all the photos posted on social media by the war reporters Poddubny, Kots, Kozlyuk, Kushnir, Sidash, and Parfenyuk. There's a chance the missing boy might have ended up in one of their photos. Then they could determine the location of that photo, find out which humanitarian organizations are operating there, and figure out where the boy was taken. They could study the chatrooms of the volunteers from the Russian or Ukrainian orphanage where the boy ended up, and they'd find the boy. After that, if he's located in Russia, it's the job of the Children's Rights representatives to make sure that that Ukrainian boy is returned to Ukraine.

For now, searching through the enormous amount of data collected from social media is still being done by hand. But the Conflict Intelligence Team has already created a bot to help with the preliminary analysis of information. For now, many journalist researchers, like the legendary Christ Grozev from the Bellingcat Group, are being prosecuted in Russia and labelled enemies. For now, information regarding the movement of troops and war crimes is being gathered through radio intercepts, satellite photographs, tracking data, and by hackers who can break into the inboxes of the generals. With just a bit of speculation, it's not difficult to imagine that very soon such investigations will be conducted not by people but by computer algorithms. If in technologically-advanced authoritarian countries, like China, the state already knows how to carry out the total surveillance of its citizens, how to recognize their faces on the street, awarding loyalty points for trustworthiness and detracting points for debauchery and rebellious behavior, then we can assume that in the very near future mankind will learn how to identify all the war criminals and how to establish who exactly fired this particular bullet to kill this particular person, and on whose orders.

And that hypothetical computer won't be overwhelmed by such an enormous amount of data. The question here is not so much whether a computer algorithm is able to process a sea of military information, but whether a smart machine will have any desire to restore the justice that human beings have undermined so brutally.

When the Ukrainian Security Service talks about "working with" the women who were raped in Bucha, it's clear they're not just referring to doctors and psychologists but to collecting DNA samples. It seems totally impossible to find a rapist among thousands of enemy soldiers right now—and the rapists count on that. But the world is changing, and human DNA registries are being compiled in all the developed countries. From a medical point of view, it's a very useful enterprise. Because when the DNA of hundreds of millions of people worldwide is registered, it becomes possible to find, for example, bone marrow donors for cancer patients. It becomes possible to design an individual course of treatment for a patient. It becomes possible to fix genetic mutations that for centuries were a curse for certain blood lines, if not for entire nations. Today, personal DNA information is considered private and protected by law, but most futurologists believe that in less than fifty years everyone on the Earth will agree to open their DNA code—as it can literally save you from death and prolong life for decades.

People will open their DNA codes at least to doctors, and then a computer will detect that the young soldier who raped a woman in Bucha in 2022 and the old man being treated in a hospital for prostate cancer 50 years from now is the same person.

They will find you, soldier! You must have skipped biology in school if you don't understand that you will be found. In ten, twenty, or even fifty years, the children and grandchildren of Ukrainian refugees will witness court cases brought against the criminals from the Ukrainian war of 2022.

The question here is not whether the criminologists who came to Bucha from all over the world will be able to solve the crimes committed there—sooner or later, they will. The question is not whether they will determine who bombed that convoy carrying medications near Chernigov, where Alexandra Volgina's friends perished—sooner or later, they will. The real question is whether ten, twenty, or fifty years from now we will feel the same sympathy for the victims in Bucha and Chernigov as we do now. The ultimate question, therefore, is whether these findings will matter to anyone.

Millions of False Testimonies

Unfortunately, most people have short emotional memory, and political strategists and PR specialists take advantage of this fact. A true story about victims of a ten-year-old crime evokes less compassion in people than a false story about today's victims.

Consider a video of a refugee from Mariupol. She says that she wasn't running from Russian bombing but from the atrocities committed by the Azov Battalion soldiers, those with the insignia. This poor woman is so sympathetic, one has to be a total monster not to feel sorry for her. Like it or not, you start believing that everyone becomes a monster during war. But a few days pass, and experts have now thoroughly studied the story's metadata, making it clear that the refugee's story, if not completely false, is heavily edited—it was filmed several times, then the footage was cut and reassembled.

The problem here is that the story about the atrocities of the Azov Battalion soldiers makes a direct emotional impact on the viewers, and most people don't even know what metadata is all about. The woman crying on the screen touches our emotions, but the expert explaining for twenty minutes why this video is a fake doesn't touch us at all. The emotional story of the refugee generates waves of responses across the Internet, while the analysis of the expert doesn't garner any reaction at all.

And it's not only political masterminds who instigate informational waves and it's not only PR specialists from Moscow who take advantage of them to ignite hostility between Eastern and Western Ukrainians in Donbas. Sometimes, very decent people spread fake or excessively exaggerated information out of the best intentions.

When the Ukrainian army freed Bucha and cases of raped children were uncovered and documented, the entire world froze in horror. It seemed that right then, at that very moment, in the wake of the most disturbing crime imaginable, the war would stop. It seemed that the soldiers would be so horrified, they would lay down their weapons. But the war didn't stop. And then the news of other documented cases of child rape began to multiply on social media. More often and with less proof, Lyudmila Denisova, the Ukrainian Commissioner for Human Rights, began announcing cases of child rape. Sexual offenses against children in Ukraine began to be labelled a mass crime, until it became clear that most of the cases were not confirmed. Ultimately, the Ukrainian parliament, the Verkhovna Rada, had to dismiss the Commissioner for Human Rights, stating that she had claimed too many unproven cases of child rape and paid too little attention to organizing humanitarian corridors for the refugees.

It should be noted that the unsupported claims of Russian soldiers raping children in the occupied territories of Ukraine not only discredited the Ukrainian authorities in the ongoing informational war but also diluted with terabytes of lies the real tragedies of the children who actually suffered such violence.

Do you remember Dr. Evgeny Pinelis, the one who brought Plan B contraceptives to Przemyśl and contemplated the number of women who had been raped in Ukraine if every American volunteer doctor was bringing a box full of morning-after pills?

I once witnessed how the topic of sexual violence displaced all other conversations in the Rubikus volunteer chatroom. A volunteer wrote that a group of Ukrainian volunteers was looking for birth control pills. Someone answered that the American doctors might have Plan B pills. Someone else answered that the American doctors didn't have any contraceptives because all the pills had been sent to Ukraine. And this is when the discussions started—about abortion being illegal in Poland, about the feminist organizations that help women get abortions in Austria, and about the rape statistics from previous wars. The moderator had to interrupt and call the volunteers to order, reminding them that the chatroom was there to help refugees leave Ukraine, not to discuss the problem of violence toward women, no matter how serious the problem might be. The idle Internet noise that presents violence as an almost everyday occurrence in war devalues the tragedy of women who were raped by the soldiers of the occupation army.

Another issue became widely discussed at about the same time. In May on European social networks and in June on Russian sites, discussion of human trafficking was raging. These discussions went as far as surmising that any man arriving in Przemyśl in his own car to give refugees a ride must be a pimp seeking to take young Ukrainian women straight to one of the brothels on Reeperbah in Hamburg or to the Red Light District in Amsterdam. Several volunteers confided in me that they'd left the refugee camps because they couldn't stand seeing a line of cars whose drivers were looking for any opportunity to kidnap beautiful Ukrainian girls for sex trafficking. One might easily assume there were pimps and human traffickers among the volunteer drivers, but it would be no more than a few people among the many thousands of volunteers. Most people who were waiting at the border were, of course, honest men who just wanted to help. Among the ten million refugees who arrived in Europe, I know of only two cases when police got involved, suspecting a volunteer driver of human trafficking. I'm not saying that there were no cases of human trafficking. What I'm saying is that we shouldn't exaggerate the number of cases. There's a ton of evidence, and all the victims will be found.

By the beginning of summer, when the number of people fleeing Ukraine to Russia or through Russia to Europe totaled over a million, users of Russian social media networks started seeing a growing number of ads of a sexual nature—"Want to meet a pretty refugee girl for serious relationship," "Will rent half of a couch in Voronezh to a refugee girl," and so on, with a greater or lesser degree of male chauvinism and impropriety.

The publishing house *Vyorstka* has even investigated the topic. The female journalists from *Vyorstka* found forty-five ads from men seeking women refugees as wives, servants, or concubines. But they found only one woman who actually answered such an ad, but there was no violence of any kind, only wasted time—she didn't like the man and left. But those are only forty-five cases out of a million! It would seem that the sexual exploitation of powerless women refugees doesn't present a significant social problem. And if there is such a problem, it too will be investigated. There are millions of witnesses, so we shouldn't imagine things that never happened. The enormous number of fabricated refugee tragedies spreading across the Internet is even more maddening as there is no lack of real tragedies. Ten million refugees amount to ten million tragedies.

Ilya Novikov, a prominent Russian lawyer who lives and works in Kyiv, reacted to the outbreak of war by enlisting in the militia—the Territorial Defense. Ilya had a large van that was a big help in transporting humanitarian aid, especially in the early days of the war. But after Bucha was liberated, Ilya went back to his original occupation and began collecting evidence of war crimes, focusing on violence against civilians. Novikov is a brilliant lawyer, so he is not interested in just any evidence—he collects only reliable proof, the kind that will hold up in court. He's not interested in just any videos but only those with a clear provenance—that is, when there's a person who can testify under the oath: "Yes, I took this video at this location at that time." I have absolutely no doubt that in several months Novikov will have put together a comprehensive archive of reliable evidence for the future war crimes tribunal for the Ukrainian war of 2022. The archives are for the courts and for the international tribunal, but not for human hearts. People need stories about people.

My Refugee

I'm absolutely convinced that despite the importance of court verdicts, they aren't very effective in preventing future wars. Empathy, pity, and compassion are much better at that. I believe that few soldiers would be capable of pulling the trigger if, at that moment, they imagined standing before them someone like themselves, a woman as their mother, and a child as their son or daughter.

Am I naïve? Didn't someone shoot children in the back in Mariupol? Didn't someone execute people who had been tied up by firing into the back of their heads? In the spinal cord. In the occiputs.

Even for the cruelest person, I believe it's hard to kill another human being while looking into that person's eyes. It's hard to keep fighting a war if you personally know refugees of that war.

I have no actual proof that I'm right, but there are a few things that support my belief in the power of eye contact.

I remember times in Soviet society when it was customary to avoid children with cancer and wish them a speedy end to their suffering—and our inconvenience. But the actress Chulpan Khamatova began taking these children on stage with her, and those attitudes began to change—people fell in love with those kids, and it became possible to successfully treat them.

I remember how HIV-positive people were considered untouchables and some felt comfortable enough to suggest their extermination. But Alexandra Volgina and her friends showed their faces, told their stories, and attitudes began to change.

I remember how a group of intellectuals in Petersburg began publishing a newspaper that was distributed by homeless people. People had to buy the most interesting newspaper of that period, *Na Dne*, from homeless people. And gradually people got used to the thought that the homeless are people too.

I think the main purpose of this book is to give people the chance to imagine that on enemy territory there are people too. Regardless what side of the firing line you're on.

I believe that to stop this war in your heart, you have to begin by having your own personal refugee—an acquaintance whose life was destroyed by the geo-political ambitions of my country. That's why I'm entering a building adjacent to a popular café on one of the central streets of Riga, not far from the railway station. I take the elevator to the fifth floor. This is the hostel, a way station where Rubikus brings refugees traveling via the Northern Stream—through Russia to Sweden and Germany. People will spend a night or two in this place, waiting for their ferry tickets or paperwork, and then continue on. The Latvian government runs a modest program to help refugees, but its state centers for refugees accept only those who are going to stay in Latvia. There is no place for transit refugees, and that's why Rubikus rented this entire hostel for them.

It's worth pointing out that the owner of this hostel is Indian. Of course, he receives money, but he is sincerely trying to help the refugees, and his help goes well beyond any rental agreement. A guy from India welcomes Ukrainian refugees in Latvia with money collected by Russian volunteers in America, Great Britain, Germany, Israel, and Russia—this is what I see as the alternative to inter-ethnic wars.

The hostel space is rather crowded. There are four bunkbeds in every room, providing sleeping places for eight. The first room I enter is occupied by people who already know one another—they're former neighbors from Goptivka village in the Kharkiv region, right on the Russian border. This village was the first one occupied by the Russian army on February 24. They fled in June from the shelling that is now coming from Ukrainian artillery.

"We get it, they have to free our homeland," says a man of about fifty. "The Russians live in our houses, so how else can you kick them out? We get it, of course, but a hundred forty strikes a day makes it impossible to live there."

This man's name is Oleg. He's tall and slim, with gray hair and a stoop. There are two very old gold teeth in his mouth. He's a mechanic who used to work in Kharkiv. His wife Lyuba is sitting by the window. Next to her is their neighbor Larisa who worked as a custodian in a Kharkiv school. She used to have a mini-farm next to her house. In Goptivka, everyone had a few fruit trees, a vegetable patch, a chicken coop, and maybe a pig or two. Larisa says that right before the war the roosters were crowing very loudly, in a high-pitched furious tone. Everyone noticed it. And right before the war a ferret came and killed all the chickens. Larisa is certain that the ferret and the chicken were trying to warn her, but she didn't get it. Right before the Ukrainian counterattack, sometime in May, a snake went crawling by—it too was trying to warn Larisa. But the woman still didn't understand that this was a sign, and she killed the snake: *Now I see I shouldn't have done that.*

When the Russians came, the first thing they did was lay

mines everywhere except under the paved streets. Oleg says they even tried to mine the well, and he and his neighbors had to argue with the enemy's sappers: *What are you doing! This is a well—people need water!* Strangely enough, the sappers listened and demined the well. But the mine fields remain in the woods, fields, and meadows, which made it impossible to even think about planting in the spring.

Oleg says there was a Chechen division staying in Goptivka—maybe they were suppliers, or maybe a communications unit. Maybe they weren't even Chechens, but they were definitely Muslims—they didn't eat pork; their canned meat was always beef. The soldiers settled in the villagers' houses, and the civilians began to leave. As people left, they released their livestock. There were now cows, goats, and pigs roaming everywhere, occasionally stepping on a mine and exploding. Homeless dogs formed packs and started hunting homeless chickens and rabbits. When Oleg and his neighbors decided to leave, they asked Russian soldiers for help, the same soldiers that had tried to mine their well. And the soldiers helped them, getting hold of a military truck and taking them to the Belgorod region.

It's good there were young people in that truck. Oleg doesn't know much about social media. Larisa doesn't have a clue. She can't even imagine how one can move through an unknown city just by looking at a screen or order tickets to a ferry through a volunteer in America. All this is significantly more complicated than deciphering the meaning behind a ferret or a snake. So, it's good there were young people in the group. They contacted volunteers, the volunteers collected money, bought tickets, and the group was able to leave. Through Petersburg, Narva, Riga, they traveled to Germany, where it seems their compatriots were working at some plant that produces beer.

They want to find work. Oleg says, even if the war is over by winter, it will be impossible to go back to Goptivka. The village is destroyed; there are no people left. Out of the six hundred people who used to live there, only sixty remain, maybe even fewer. The area is mined, and it will take months to clear the mines. There are no construction materials to rebuild their homes, and it's unlikely any will be available in the near future; therefore, they have to look for jobs in whichever place their long journey takes them.

Petersburg impressed them the most. The volunteer who met the Goptivka crew at the railway station took them to her home on Vasilyevsky Island. They were surprised that the streets on Vasilyevsky Island were called lines. Their volunteer lived with her family—her mother and her young children. Oleg and Lyuba felt like they had arrived at a relative's place to spend the night. The next morning, they went on a walk through the city and climbed up the stairs of St. Isaac's Cathedral. The view was breathtaking. They couldn't grasp how a country with such beautiful cities and such kind people could . . . But Oleg tries not to think about that.

The driver who picked them up the next day to take them from Petersburg to Narva was a very kind person too. After two hours of driving, he parked the car on the side of the road and announced a sanitary stop. "Girls to the right, boys to the left," he said and began walking toward the woods. Oleg ran after him, grabbed his arm, almost knocking him down: "Where are you going? There are mines!" And then he realized that there were probably no mines in the Leningrad region. Oleg realized that Narva and Riga weren't mined either, but when the volunteers suggested they go for a walk, he chose to stay inside the car.

There was also a *babushka* among the Goptivka refugees, Oleg's mother-in-law. The volunteers gave her a gift, a folding chair, so she could sit during the long filtration process on the Russian-Estonian border. The volunteers determined ahead of time whether there was a need for folding chairs by asking if there were any old people in the group who might find it difficult to stand for a long period of time. It was hard to grasp how one nation could produce people who thought about a folding chair for an old woman and people who . . . But Oleg tries not to think about that.

In Narva, there was a bus waiting to take them to Riga, where they were fed and sheltered for two days. Then they'd be taken to the ferry to Liepāja . . .

When Oleg talks about the folding chair, the buses, and the hostel, he seems to understand where the money is coming from, but seems unable to figure out what I've been doing there in that hostel.

All this time I've been committing everything to memory. I remember Oleg, Lyuba, and Larisa, and I also remember Alla, Denys, Lena, Vika, Alyona and Andrey, Lyubov Alexandrovna and Nikolay Petrovich. I remember Oksana number one and Oksana number two. Ira-Roma, little Danilka—I remember them all. And when the Ukrainian cities are bombed, I imagine not some abstract civilians but them—my friends, these refugees whom I know by face and by name.

Chapter 11
The New Face of Femininity

> "The Russian Ministry of Defense together with the Union of Russian Women is carrying out the humanitarian action 'A Care Package to a Soldier. To Our Z-Defenders with Love' in support of those participating in the Special Military Operation. The committees of the Union of Russian Women are helping to collect humanitarian aid for refugees and residents of the Donbass. A total of over 495 tons of essentials, food and household goods has been sent."
> The Official Telegram Channel of the Russian Ministry of Defense, April 14, 2022.

A Loss of Orientation

I don't really know how significant this fact is (in my humble opinion, it's important), but Anastasiya Chukovskaya comes from a very good family. One of her great-grandfathers is the world-famous composer Dmitry Shostakovich, another—the great children's poet Korney Chukovsky. In addition to these two cornerstones of modern Russian culture, there are so many famous writers, scientists, musicians, and athletes in her family, it's hard to remember all of them.

Anastasiya spent her early years in the US, and at some point her English was more fluent than her Russian. In her head, the great works of American literature got mixed up with the great works of Russian literature. In a word, Nastya, in some mysterious sense, is the complete opposite of the typical Russian soldier who invaded Ukraine. He is without roots, while Nastya's family tree reaches back for God only knows how many generations. He's been poor his entire life, while Nastya has always been well off, even in the least successful periods of her life. He hasn't seen anything outside his village, while Nastya's seen the entire world. He hasn't read a single book; while, after talking with Nastya, it's hard to name a book she hasn't read. To finish up this list of differences, is it even necessary to add that the occupying soldier is a man, while Nastya is a woman?

In the mid-1990s, she was studying at Moscow State University, in the Department of Journalism, which was one of the most interesting places in the world at that time. She then worked at some of the most popular magazines and newspapers in Russia, all of which are now closed. Back in the 90s, these publications were full of hope for a new Russia; now they're outlawed because they promoted peace, which became illegal in the Russia of the 2020s.

In 2011, when the democratic protests in Moscow failed, Nastya and her family moved to Budapest. But when she emigrated, she didn't leave her circle—those friends who were trying to build a beautiful Russia of the future, about which we were all fantasizing as Russia's present grew increasingly dark. Nastya was working for Yandex, one of the most progressive and technologically advanced Russian companies, where she was in charge of its most innovative projects—organizing schools for creative thinking in the Russian provinces. But then the war began.

February 24 found Nastya Chukovskaya in Moscow on a business trip. Her first thought was to buy a ticket and return immediately to her children in Budapest. She left on February 25 on one of the last direct flights from a half-empty airport on a half-empty plane. The stream of emigrants had yet to form. In those first days of the war, almost no one in Russia could assess the scale of the catastrophe; everyone thought that Kyiv would be occupied within a couple of days, as had recently occurred in Tbilisi. Of course, everyone would be deeply ashamed of their country, but they'd been ashamed of it several times already and had somehow gotten used to it.

When Nastya left the airport in Budapest, she felt a sense of relief. Only now, after the war began, did she realize that it had always been scary to live in Russia. Before the 24th, this fear wasn't tangible, but after the 24th it felt like the very air in Russia was slightly poisoned by fear, the atmosphere in Russia was filled with it; it was like molten lead, and nothing could be done, no resistance was possible. But step outside the airport in Budapest, and the darkness subsides. Nastya thought she'd started feeling normal again after returning to Budapest. The next day, Nastya took her son to school. It was a familiar route: two stops on one tram, then change trams, and two stops on another. Nastya and her son must've taken this route a thousand times, but on that day they took the wrong tram, went in the wrong direction, then switched trams in the wrong place and took the wrong tram again. Only half an hour later did they realize they weren't in the right part of the city.

Well, it's okay, it's not the end of the world. The city is familiar, we've lived here for ten years. All we have to do is take a bus, go a couple of stops, then switch buses, and the second bus will take us to school in five minutes. Well, we'd probably be about fifteen minutes late—no big deal. They got on a bus, but again, it was the wrong one; then they switched buses in the wrong place and took another wrong bus, ending up once again in the wrong place.

Apart from confusing the public transportation routes, Nastya began noticing other unpleasant symptoms. For example, she noticed that she'd become completely incapable of reading books. On top of that, she would put the kitchen utensils away in the wrong place so that no one could find them. In a word, she had suddenly become disoriented.

And if she was that disoriented after leaving the comfort of Moscow, which hasn't experienced any bombing, and while living in a familiar city in a house with her husband and children, then how disorienting must it be for those refugees who are fleeing bombardment in Kharkiv, Kyiv, or Mykolaiv and traveling into the complete unknown?

At about the same time, Nastya received a call from an unknown number:

"Hello. Galina gave me your phone number. She said you might be able to help me in Budapest, possibly."

Nastya had no idea who that Galina was, but after a couple of sentences it became clear that the caller was a refugee. And suddenly, Nastya's disorientation was gone.

Nastya, who only yesterday believed she needed psychiatric help, suddenly realized that her post-traumatic disorientation could be successfully treated by helping other people. And she got to work.

The first thing she and her husband did was remove all the musical instruments and recording equipment from her husband's three-room studio to set up a temporary shelter for refugees. Nastya's husband didn't mind losing his studio and was happy to help his wife. But keep in mind: The idea came into Nastya's head, not her husband's.

Every day they would go to the railroad station to meet refugees arriving on Ukrainian trains. They would take them to the apartment and feed them with provisions brought by other volunteers. They would create itineraries to direct the refugees farther along, then bring home from the train station new refugees, and post about them on social media, asking for help. And people began offering help. A total stranger called her from London. The woman introduced herself as Yelena and informed Nastya that she had rented an entire hotel for Nastya's refugees—a medium size hotel located near the train station. The number of Nastya's refugees kept increasing, and they needed more food and clothes. So, she had to continue posting about the refugees on social media. An unknown Lyuda called from Seattle and asked where exactly the apartment where Nastya and her husband were housing refugees was located. After learning the address, she rented an apartment in the building next door so it would be easier for

Nastya and her volunteer friends to provide the refugees with food and clothes.

Thanks to Nastya's posts on social media, money started to arrive from both private donors and from companies. Nastya compiled a list of empty apartments—there are many in Budapest—and asked the owners to let refugees stay in them.

The number of transit refugees was decreasing. But there were more and more refugees who wanted to stay in Budapest. This was easy to explain: The refugees couldn't believe they would be away from Ukraine for very long. They thought that in a month or two, okay, maybe three, they'd be able to return home. Many of them didn't even bother to get their refugee papers or apply for refugee status and social assistance because they hoped their savings would be enough for them to wait out the war. Of the one million refugees that entered Hungary, only twenty-four thousand officially registered. Some of them, of course, traveled on, but many stayed and waited. For Ukrainian refugees, it wasn't so scary to wait in Hungary—it was only three hours by train to their homeland. It's very comforting to think you can easily go back home.

In addition to temporary lodgings, it became necessary to rent more permanent accommodations for those refugees who decided to stay and wait. And this seemed totally normal to Nastya. What surprised her was something else. Nastya couldn't understand why the problem of refugees had become so important to her only now, why she now felt like it was her calling in life, when several years ago whole families of Syrian refugees were living in cardboard boxes in underground crossings, and Nastya simply walked past them. Well, she might give them some money or bring used clothes for their kids, but she didn't rent them apartments or give them her husband's studio . . . Why? Because they're Muslims? Because they're dark-skinned? Because they speak a language she doesn't know? For some reason, the stream of refugees from Ukraine made Nastya re-evaluate her attitude toward refugees in general—whether they're from Syria or from Mars.

There was another problem with the Ukrainian refugees: Most of them were women with children. But in Hungary, as in any other country, landlords try their best to avoid renting apartments to women with children because you can't evict them. Even if a woman hasn't paid rent for an entire year, the law prohibits the eviction of a woman with a child. So, without local infrastructure, without Hungarian citizens willing to rent apartments under their names or co-signing the lease, refugees would have to live in temporary refugee centers in remodeled gyms, shopping centers, and incidentally, the temporary COVID hospitals that had now become available. On the other hand, how many apartments can a Hungarian citizen rent under their name and how many leases can one Hungarian citizen co-sign? How long will it take until the refugees they decided to help bring them to the brink of bankruptcy? Even though Nastya's posts on social media had brought in significant donations, how much longer would these donations continue?

Gradually it became clear that without the help of governments and major charity funds, Nastya's efforts would have to cease.

Legos Are Not for Eating

Lilya called next. Nastya had already gotten used to unknown people calling her and asking for something. But Lilya wasn't asking for anything. It seems that she, like Nastya, had figured out that the best remedy for post-traumatic stress syndrome was helping others. Lilya was actively searching for a Ukrainian school in Budapest where Ukrainian children could continue their studies and Ukrainian refugee teachers could start working again. Lilya herself was a teacher, as was her friend with whom she'd fled Kyiv.

What?! There's no Ukrainian school? That can mean only one thing—we need to organize one.

And Lilya began organizing just such a school. In a few days she found seventy students who were ready then and there to continue their education. And she found fifteen teachers ready to begin teaching right away. Nastya's role in organizing the school was mainly managerial: locating a building, finding money to pay the teachers' salaries, and obtaining a license so the grades the kids would receive at the end of the school year would count and they could register for the next grade in their homeland or anywhere else. And then there'd be summer. Which means they'd have to organize a summer camp so the kids wouldn't be idle but would have something fun, useful, and therapeutic to do. Everything came together in a few days. A rich man living in Dubai gave Nastya the entire floor of the business-center he owned for her Ukrainian school. Other sponsors came forward—big companies and individuals.

Little by little, the educational problems were resolved. It's not that easy to organize a Ukrainian school in Hungary. Where do you get the textbooks? How do you adjust the curriculum? Should it be adjusted to the fact that everyone around them speaks Hungarian? Should it be adjusted to the fact that there's a war in their homeland, or should they just ignore it? How should they deal with the post-traumatic stress disorder that virtually all their students are experiencing? How should they teach history that only a month ago had pulled the children into its deadly vortex? Eventually answers were found and problems were solved.

The only outstanding problem was getting the school officially certified so the teachers wouldn't have to be paid under the table but could receive real salaries in accordance with the Payroll and Job Description Schedule, and so the students would receive a real diploma instead of a certificate for having audited some classes. Nastya realized that, although one could feed and shelter refugees without registering as a legal entity, teaching refugees and creating jobs for them was totally different. You can't run such a business without being legally registered. In order for the school to function, it would be necessary to find an official charity fund willing to take the school under its wing—Nastya couldn't think of any other way to legalize her school.

Nastya tells me how the negotiations with the charity funds took more of her time than settling all the refugees. One fund was ready to handle the rental documents but didn't want to deal with the teachers' paperwork. Another was ready to work with the teachers but refused to deal with real estate. A third worked only with personal donations so refused to deal with donations from corporate sponsors and the government. A fourth was ready to accept grants from government and international organizations but didn't want to deal with measly private donations, even if they amounted in the end to huge sums of money. And on the top of that, the first fund refused to work with the third, the third insisted that it could work with all the funds except the first, the second didn't want to work with anybody, and every fund expected that Nastya's school project would be adjusted to meet their particular rules and regulations.

After long negotiations, a charity fund was located that was willing to accept the building Nastya had found, the money Nastya had raised, and the staff Nastya had put together. The school opened and soon gained a very positive reputation. The reviews were so good that the UNICEF representative came to observe the school's achievements. They led her through the classrooms and showed her the children, after which the representative of UNICEF and the representative of the charity fund retreated to a conference room to discuss important matters. Neither Lilya, who created and ran the school, nor Nastya, who organized and financed the school, were invited to that meeting. As Nastya remarks, it must be the working style of international charity funds: solving the problems of patients without patients, and the problems of refugees—without refugees.

The organization of the summer camp went much smoother. The Lego company helped. One of Nastya's friends worked for the company. She worked in Munich, but her grandmother, who was elderly and in poor health, lived in the Ukrainian city of Dnipro. So, the Lego company helped their employee evacuate her grandma, and the help needed was significant: The company sent an ambulance to bring the grandmother to Munich and rented rooms in decent hotels along the way.

And along the way it turned out that Lego had an entire series of educational programs based on their construction toys, which children all over the world love to play with. It turned out that it was possible not only to play with toys, but also to learn through playing. It turned out that for every Lego toy—from spacecraft and Medieval castles to simple cubes for toddlers—a lesson has been developed, and there are teaching programs and people familiar with these programs who are ready to teach other instructors.

In a word, the camp was a success, and everyone was happy with it. The kids loved that the program consisted mainly of Lego games; the parents loved that their children were supervised, which gave them some free time to complete paperwork and look for jobs; and Nastya loved that they finally had not only a Ukrainian school but also a Ukrainian summer camp. But the happiest of all was Nastya's friend who worked for Lego. She used to see her job only as a source of income, but now she was sure that by working for Lego she was making this world a better place. And she promised herself to work for Lego all her life, no matter how much more she might make at other companies.

There's only one problem with Nastya's partner, Lego: You can't eat Lego bricks.

This World's Gone Mad

Nastya's motto for working with refugees is: "It shouldn't be like this—it should be different."

By the end of summer, a million people had crossed the Hungarian border but only twenty-four thousand had gotten registered—*It shouldn't be like this, we need to find these people and help them.* The Hungarian state allocated seventy euros a month to every adult refugee and forty for every child refugee. But in Hungary, most Ukrainian refugees haven't received even this subsistence aid. *It shouldn't be like this. They suffer from hunger. Food is a human right!*

In the city of Kecskemét, the refugees find jobs at the Samsung factory. The company provides them with living accommodations. But what kind of accommodations are they?! They're in an abandoned building, where no one has lived for many years and all communication infrastructure is destroyed. Not only are pets not allowed in the building but neither are children. In order to have a job and a place to live, people have to give their children to volunteers or to other refugees, their comrades in misfortune. So, the refugees form groups: They rent a more or less decent apartment for one of five or ten women, and this woman lives there with ten children while the others live in the Samsung dorm and work. *It shouldn't be like this! Help shouldn't be provided on the condition that children are separated from their parents.*

"This dorm in Kecskemét," Nastya begins. She pauses but then decides to come right out and say it, "It looks like a prison. It's surrounded by wasteland, there's no place to play ball or even to sit on a bench. There are guards at the entrance, and no visitors are allowed inside." To deliver food to the refugees, Nastya and her friends must stop at the entrance, unload their packages with food, and then the refugees come out and take the food inside. What does it look like inside? Why are neither volunteers nor journalists allowed to see the living conditions of the refugees? Are the conditions so terrible? *It shouldn't be like this! It should be done more humanely.*

The situation is similar with the dorm at the meat-processing plant. The work at this plant is very difficult and poorly paid, but the refugees can't afford to leave because they'd lose their place to live. And how many dorms like this are there? Nastya wrote to the UN High Commission and asked them to provide her with a list of all the refugee dormitories in Hungary. But the High Commission didn't answer and, as far as Nastya knows, there's only one Ukrainian on this Commission. That seems to be the approach of the international organizations: They decide the refugees' problems without refugees and the Ukrainians' problems without Ukrainians. *It shouldn't be like this.*

When the war began, Europe was very enthusiastic about helping Ukraine. For ninety days, all public transportation in Europe was free for refugees; they established a payment system and free medical insurance for refugees; in supermarkets, regular people bought food not only for themselves but also for refugees and they would leave this food in the charity carts at the door. But ninety days had passed. The stream of refugees wasn't slowing down. Moreover, the refugees who came to Europe in March were fleeing the bombardment of cities that were not yet destroyed, and so they had time to pack and could bring at least some clothes. By May and June, the refugees were fleeing ruins, arriving in Europe sick and injured, without clothes and without papers.

But Europe got tired. Germany discontinued free transportation and offered a travel pass instead—it's not expensive, but you still need to have money to buy it. Czechia decreased the amount of its payments. Hungary didn't fulfill their promises. No one is standing with charity carts at supermarkets anymore. Nastya has a hard time convincing her Facebook subscribers to keep buying food for the refugees.

People got tired of refugees. More and more people on social media and even from parliamentary rostrums are saying: *Why should we help refugees when our own citizens are living below the poverty line* (eight hundred thousand in Hungary)? Many say: *Why do we have to house refugees in apartments when our Romas live in tents?* Thank God, they finally thought about the Romas! And about the poor! A war had to break out in Europe for people to finally take notice of the less fortunate and reassess the fairness of their own society and the stability of their own well-being.

Nastya sincerely believes that this particular war and this particular stream of refugees should change our perception of the world. If we allowed this war to happen, then it's a mistake to think that only the people from the regions directly affected by the war should have to deal with its consequences. In reality, a war affects at least all the countries bordering the conflict's border, but to be honest, it affects all mankind.

In reality, the refugee assistance funds should not be determined according to the budgets of countries and international organizations; it should be done in the opposite direction—the budgets of countries and international organizations should be determined so as to accommodate the needs of refugees. Let's stop thinking of refugees living on cardboard boxes in underground crossings as normal.

If we believe that refugees have the right to live in apartments similar to ours, to eat basically the same food as our families eat, to wear comparable clothes, to study in our schools, to get medical help in our hospitals—if we believe this and do everything we can to find the money to make this possible, then we won't have any money left for wars.

And we'll have to believe this. If not during this nightmare, then during the next. If not now when people are fleeing bombardment in Ukraine, then in six months, when people will be fleeing Africa due to the famine caused by the Russian blockade of Ukrainian ports where the wheat bound for Africa is stored.

We'll have to believe that refugees are not an annoying burden, not the dirty-faced inhabitants of underground crossings and tent cities whom we can pass by without noticing. We must believe that refugees are part of a new reality. They can do jobs that their hosts don't know how to do. Their experience of suffering can make us all kinder, better people. Furthermore, they have their beautiful folk songs and their delicious national cuisines. They can enrich the country that accepts them.

We must realize one thing. This world has gone mad. War is spreading. Maybe not today, but tomorrow every person, even the most secure in the world, can become a refugee. We must understand this. And after this realization settles in, we need to imagine how we would like to be treated by others when we become refugees.

You don't think you could become a refugee? Go back to the beginning of this book—not one of its characters planned to become a refugee. They were all successful, well-off professionals—scientists, businessmen, artists, and farmers. None of them imagined such a twist of fate.

As it happens, anyone can become a refugee. Even a citizen of the country whose army created the refugee crisis.

All People Are Refugees

And one more thing: I don't know if you've noticed, but all characters in this chapter are women. In this entire book, most of the characters are women, with only a few exceptions. That's how it always works: Men begin wars, and women have to deal with the consequences. As Nastya Chukovskaya would say, *It shouldn't be this way*.

Another notable feature of this war is that women are not just humbly and quietly dealing with the consequences. Perhaps not since the legendary Lysistrata have women raised their voices and taken action to such a degree. They are guiding refugees through Europe, finding them decent apartments, organizing decent schools for them, and treating them in decent hospitals. They've even organized Think Tanks at various universities throughout the world. Taking part in one such think tank is Yulia Leytes—remember her, the psychologist and feminist who was walking during the bombardment in Kyiv trying not to notice the war? During these Think Tanks, women scientists from different countries discuss how to organize the future of a world that men have failed, leaving women to pick up the debris and manage the crisis.

When Oleksiy Arestovich, the Strategic Communications Adviser for the Office of the President of Ukraine, talks about the war, he defines masculinity as the ability to act when you want to flee. Then how do we define femininity? As the ability to strive for the unrealistic because the unreal has become the new normal? As the ability to help when you need help yourself? To sympathize when you yourself need sympathy the most? How is a female world designed? How does this world make ends meet? We know how the male world is designed. In a male world, it's normal to spend billions on armaments and then spend pennies on keeping refugees in tent cities. How would it be in a female world? Billions spent on refugees? But where will these billions come from? Nastya Chukovskaya is positive this money will come from people. Not by raising taxes, but when people realize it's necessary to put money aside for emergencies not only for their own family but for the emergencies faced by refugees who arrive from a country destroyed by war.

In talking with my female heroines, I seem to have stumbled on an economic model where the humane accommodation of refugees becomes possible. All my heroines believe in social networks, in other words, in the power of horizontal communication. They believe there's a place in this world for every person, even for one who has survived by some miracle the bombing of their house and who has nothing left but the ripped t-shirt on their back. There's a place for every person where they will be welcomed and treated as family. We just need to find such places, which is precisely what social networks were designed to do.

For the soil scientist Alla Achasova a place will be found at the University of Prague, a green energy specialist will be welcomed in Andorra, a loving sister is waiting for the nurse Yelena Chepurnaya in Cyprus—all we have to do is find a place for everybody. My heroines believe that such places exist.

But I don't believe it. I think the world these women are trying to create, the world where there's no difference between refugees and hosts, can exist only under one condition: If the war spreads to the entire world and all people become refugees.

Chapter 12
Double Enemies

> "Foreign journalists arrived in the city to prepare photos and videos of civilians supposedly 'murdered by Russians' and to circulate them widely on Ukrainian and western social media." Official Telegram Channel of the Russian Ministry of Defense, August 6, 2022.

Read This in the Event They Put Me in Front of a Firing Squad

It's not that difficult to become a refugee, even if you're a citizen of the aggressor country. You just have to be like Lena.

Here's Lena carrying a heavy bag. A very heavy bag. In the bag is a bulletproof vest and a helmet. Lena is slender—just a wisp of a thing. Elena Kostyuchenko (her full name) is an extremely courageous reporter for the newspaper *Novaya Gazeta*. She's famous for her amazing, thoroughly detailed reporting from all around the world on the nightmare of war and revolution. And when a break occurred in those wars, she started reporting from Russian psychiatric institutions, where life is not much better than in prisoner-of-war camps.

In the first days of the Russian invasion of Ukraine, Lena decides to write about the war—but not from the Russian side. She'll work on the Ukrainian side of the front, going to Mykolaiv, Kherson, and Mariupol with a Russian passport, a Russian press card—and for Russian readers. As a result, she will be hated in both countries. The only problem is that it's hard to hate Lena. She's a woman of rare beauty with the body of a ballet dancer, dark hair, blue eyes, and a gentle voice. And it's hard to miss in her eyes and her voice the hurricane-like empathy she feels for all the people of the world. That's why people help her. Throughout all her wartime endeavors, the authorities—Ukrainian and Russian alike—will interfere and obstruct her efforts, but common people will help.

So, here is Lena dragging her bag with a bulletproof vest and a helmet to the border crossing at Medyka, where the border patrol officer is not looking into Lena's blue eyes—he is looking at her passport. Her passport is red—as all Russian passports are—and you can't enter Ukraine with such a passport. Lena goes back to Lublin, waits there an entire day, and talks to the refugees who have just crossed the border. These refugees had to wait in line fifteen hours in freezing weather, but they consider themselves lucky—today that line stretches to at least three days. While Lena is talking to the refugees, her boss Dmitry Muratov, the editor-in-chief of *Novaya Gazeta* and a Nobel Peace Prize winner, is calling the Ukrainian authorities and the Ukrainian Security Service from Moscow trying to persuade them to let his reporter enter their country.

The next day, Lena repeats her attempt. Again, she drags her unbearably heavy bag with a bulletproof vest and a helmet to the border checkpoint, and this time they let her cross the border into Ukraine. And with that, she enters the war zone.

After this expedition, Lena will be asked in an interview about the time she needed to get from the border to the war zone. And Lena will answer, "You don't understand what war is. War is not only when cannons are firing; war is when people's lives are destroyed." And so, the war begins in Shehyni, a Ukrainian village that sits right on the Russian border.

There are three or four thousand people in this village. Most of them are women and children. They're waiting in a long line in the freezing cold for their turn. Lena sees an elderly woman collapse from exhaustion, a child who falls asleep from the cold, and a young mother who sits down on the ground, putting her infant on her lap and covering it with her body because there is nothing else to cover it with. These are the first days of the war.

There are no volunteers yet. No blankets, no food, no campfires, but there's already a line.

Lena drags her bag with a bulletproof vest and a helmet along the road into Ukrainian territory, and after walking for about two hundred meters, she loses the Polish cellular network she was using. But there are no Ukrainian networks. There are no buses. The cars in which men take their families to the border don't stop on their way back and don't pick up any passengers—very few people were stopping for hitchhikers in the first days of the war.

There's a man walking from the border. He's seen his family off and now he's returning home.

"Excuse me, could you let me use your Internet service for a minute?" Lena asks.

The man turns around and looks into her eyes:

"Where are you going? It's twenty-five kilometers to Mostyska."

"To what?"

"Mostyska, it's a small town."

The man takes Lena's bag, and they continue walking. In an hour, they reach a gas station.

"Are you hungry?"

Lena nods. They wait in line for almost two hours, and the man buys Lena a hotdog and coffee. Lena has no money to pay for anything—her Russian bank cards are blocked in Ukraine. All Russian cellphone numbers are already blocked too, so her phone isn't working either.

They continue on. For one, two, three hours. Only when they're near Mostyska does a volunteer who's directing traffic at the intersection blocked by cars stop a driver coming back from the border and ask him to take Lena and her fellow traveler to Lviv.

In Lviv, there's a war press-center with all the typical office equipment, communication lines, high-speed Internet, and coffee for journalists. But Lena is not allowed in this press-center. Even though many people know her there and would have certainly let her in if they could, the mayor has issued an unequivocal directive: No one with a Russian passport allowed.

"May I stand near the door? There's a Wi-Fi signal on this side of the door too."

Lena is allowed to stand near the door of the Lviv press-center. But before doing anything work-related, Lena starts looking for human rights activists, or a humanitarian mission, or a commissioner for children's rights—to tell them the border's a madhouse; there's no heat, no food, no clothes for the refugees. She finds Human Rights Watch, and they promise to inform Ukrainian social services, who have been slow to react to the humanitarian crisis. They also inform Lena that there aren't any hotel rooms left, and there are no apartments available for rent either. Human Rights Watch is willing to let Lena stay overnight—they have their headquarters in Lviv—but they need to ask their security first. Alas, no luck. As it turns out, the security protocol of the international human rights organizations doesn't allow homeless Russian journalists to stay overnight in their headquarters.

At this moment another force comes into play—not bureaucratic channels, which are totally useless in time of war, but human connections. A girlfriend of one of Lena's girlfriends brings her some money. A girlfriend of a girlfriend of a girlfriend lets Lena stay overnight. A friend of a girlfriend of a girlfriend buys her a train ticket to Odesa. Friends of the friends in Odesa let her stay with them, feeding her and helping Lena get to Mykolaiv. From Mykolaiv, Lena writes one of the first and most heartbreaking reports of this war—about civilian casualties.

About two little girls, sisters, who died when a missile struck their kitchen. Lena sees their bodies lying in the morgue. The older girl has a beautiful, carefully done manicure. Lena writes about the teachers in the orphanage. When their orphanage was evacuated, the second shift of teachers followed the children in a truck. But when the children arrived at their destination, the teachers were nowhere in sight. Later, the driver explained that Russian troops had fired a warning shot, but he didn't know what that meant and didn't stop the vehicle. So, they bombed the truck. The driver was injured, and all the teachers were killed. The children would never see them again. Lena threads these stories together, one after another, and a picture emerges—a picture of what this war really is . . . If only the soldiers read Lena Kostyuchenko. If only they realized that not every missile fired lands on "enemy infrastructure." It may hit a girl with a neat manicure or a kindergarten teacher whose pupils are waiting for her. Or *do* the soldiers realize that?

After that Lena goes to Kherson, which is already occupied by the Russian army. She leaves her bag with a bulletproof vest and a helmet in Mykolaiv along with her laptop and press-card. All she takes with her is her passport and a story—that she's trying to bring her seriously ill aunt her medications, which are impossible to find in Kherson because it is so near the front. Lena can look like a very young woman when she turns off the steely expression in her eyes, which is typical of war reporters. In any case, the soldiers at the checkpoints believe her.

From Kherson, Lena writes about how the city is greeting their "liberators." The people go to a protest rally only to find out that rallies are prohibited on the territories occupied by Russia. But she also writes about retired women who are happy to receive free humanitarian provisions. This report will never be published in *Novaya Gazeta*, which had sent Lena on this assignment—as the newspaper has been closed. But her articles are published by other publications that are now working outside Russia. For them, Lena is planning to go to Mariupol next, the site of the fiercest battle so far. At this moment, Dmitry Muratov, who's not even her boss anymore, just a friend, calls her back: *It's too dangerous to go to Mariupol. It was dangerous in Mykolaiv when it was under bombardment, but it wasn't too bad. To cross the frontline twice to Kherson and back was also very dangerous, and it's a miracle she made it. But to go to Mariupol would be total madness.* The articles Lena has published, where she talks about the civilians who were shelled, have made the Russian government very angry—they couldn't have been angrier if Lena had published the coordinates of the ammunition warehouses! So, this is the greatest military secret—that there are civilians being bombed! Muratov is sure that now, having revealed this secret, Lena will be arrested at the first checkpoint and put in front of a firing squad.

Although Lena crosses the frontline without a bulletproof vest or a helmet, or even her press-card, she keeps a secret document in a secret pocket on the bottom of her backpack—in the event she's to be executed. She will show this document to the Russian soldiers who take her to the execution site. After reading this document, she hopes they won't execute her but send her to Moscow under convoy. Prison is better that death. What's in this document, Lena won't say. Luckily, she hasn't had a chance to see if the document works.

Lena's expedition is almost over. She travels to Germany, then to Czechia, where she stays in various boarding houses that provide rooms to writers so they can write books. She receives a stipend for writers. In Europe, all journalists know that Lena is one of the most adamant opponents of this war and, of course, they understand her situation, but the bureaucrats who check her passport and the people who hear her speak on the street look at her with suspicion—she carries the passport and speaks the language of the aggressor.

At first, Lena says in various interviews that she will definitely be returning soon to Russia. The city she loves and the editorial office of her favorite newspaper are there, not to mention her mother and sister. And besides, how can she leave the country to the savages who started this war? But gradually she realizes she can't go back. As long as Russia is under its current political regime, Lena can't go back. Because under this regime, journalists who write that bombs aren't hitting "the enemy's infrastructure" will be charged and prosecuted as civilians for discrediting the army and imprisoned for up to twenty years.

The Map of the Invasion

"Taras, wake me up when the war starts," says Timur Olevsky. And with these words, he goes to bed on February 23 in his brother-in-law's apartment in Kyiv.

Timur is the editor of The Insider portal, based in Prague. For a year this portal has been writing that war is inevitable. Two days before the invasion, The Insider publishes a detailed map of the future invasion. The day before the invasion, Timur leaves detailed instructions for his colleagues—how the portal should work under conditions of war—and then catches probably the last pre-war flight from Prague to Kyiv. Why does he need to go to Kyiv? Timur can't really explain—maybe to be a part of history in the making, or something like that.

And then, on February 24 at 6:00 A.M., the news editor on duty calls Timur from Prague, waking him up:

"Get up, Timur, the war's begun. It's been going on for an hour. We let you sleep a little, but now you have to get up."

Timur can barely get up, as if he's suffering from some life-threatening disease or a severe hangover, though he hadn't had a single drink with his brother-in-law. But Timur gets up and goes to work. How is it possible to work with a war going on? Timur asks his driver to take him to Hostomel, the military airport. Hostomel is not far from Kyiv. They drive for quite a while and suddenly find themselves in the middle of a battle. Mines are exploding around their car, almost under the wheels.

Russian paratroopers are trying to capture the runway. The Ukrainian army is pushing the attackers back. And in the middle of all of this is Timur Olevsky and his driver. That's how a modern war works: You can roll into battle in a taxi—you'll just have to pay a little over the meter price.

"Where are you going?" Timur screams. "Let's get out of here!"

"You told me to take you to Hostomel," the driver responds calmly. "So, this is Hostomel."

Several seconds pass. Timur and his driver leave the battlefield and drive back to Kyiv. They see people walking on the roadside—decently dressed people who are leaving their homes, their cozy middle-class houses. They're walking along the road with their fashionable wheeled suitcases bought for traveling to some Greek island. They're leading their well-dressed children by the hand. And there are explosions going off behind them. This is why it was so important for Timur to come to Ukraine on the eve of the war—to see all this. So, he could later write: The refugees are not strangers from some far-off land—every one of us can become a refugee. Today, you have a nice house and eat warm croissants for breakfast in some trendy café, but tomorrow—you're a refugee.

Some time ago, a rather long time actually—about ten years before this Ukrainian war—a video about refugees was shown on TV. The UN had commissioned the video. It irritated Timur with its lack of realism, or so he thought at the time. He'd seen the refugees in Chechnya—dirty, exhausted people in wet slippers and blankets over their coats. But in the UN video, the refugees looked like well-off middle-class people. Timur hated that video, convinced it couldn't be accurate—he was sure that refugees were someone else, people with broken, unfortunate lives. And now Timur found himself in the middle of that video: Typical members of the upper middle class were walking along the roadside. In the near future, they might become those exhausted dirty people in slippers and blankets. From his car, Timur watches how every intersection is preparing for war. How the police and the Territorial Defense militia are building fortifications. People—the entire nation—are building fortifications. This should all be filmed and shown to the Russians—no one is looking forward to their "liberation army." People "oppressed by their Nazi government" wouldn't be building barricades against their "liberators" at every intersection.

It all must be shown, but it can't be recorded. Timur realizes he's not filming not only because he doesn't have official credentials or permission from the Ukrainian authorities but also because such images can be used by the enemy—the Russian army. In other words, Timur now considers the Russian army to be the enemy. He's taken a side. And damn objective journalism! Timur even contemplates what he would've done if Russian soldiers had entered Kyiv and reached his neighborhood. Would he get a machinegun? Would he shoot? Would he kill someone if he wasn't killed first? He might have killed someone, and then he would have been unable to go on living, knowing that he'd taken another person's life.

When it comes to the Russian soldiers, Timur's feelings are complicated. On the one hand, Timur wants them to lose the war and be held responsible for their aggression. On the other hand, it's frightening to think that they allowed that evil, animal-like force that exists in every one of us, and inside of Timur too, to rise up and grow in strength. Third, Timur feels profoundly sorry for the Russian soldiers. It's a pity they are dying here.

Poor soldiers! Russia, Timur thinks, is richer than Ukraine. Obviously. It possesses more territory, its economy is bigger, its army is bigger by magnitudes; it has more missiles, tanks, and planes. But the life of a simple Russian is significantly less comfortable than that of a simple Ukrainian. People who don't have heated bathrooms in their homes attack people who have heated bathrooms in their homes. People who live with muddy, impassable roads all year long are now invading a country where even the smallest village has paved roads. They destroy, ransack, and pillage other people's comfort. They allow avarice, jealousy, and cruelty to enter their souls; they allow evil to rise up and grow in strength inside their souls. Everyone has this dark evil force inside them, including Timur. And they perish here, the poor guys. It's commonly believed that Russia's war is imperialistic. But this is not at all the case: This war is the Huns attacking Rome, not the reverse. The Barbarians are advancing on civilization, the indigent on the wealthy. That's what Timur believes, and the Russian state opposes his beliefs not with arguments but with criminal charges and up to twenty years in prison.

In Ukraine, the thought of "poor Russian soldiers perishing on Ukrainian soil" is not welcomed either. It's quite easy for a citizen of the aggressor-country to become a refugee: All you need is to have complicated and contradictory beliefs.

During the first days of the war, there are no safe places in Kyiv, and Timur wanders. He stays overnight occasionally with friends or at the volunteer centers, which are now helping to defend the city. Almost every day, Timur is on the air talking about current events as an eyewitness. He takes part in live broadcasts about the war along with Mikhail Nacke and Alexander Plyuschev, former reporters of the now shuttered radio station Ekho Moskvy.

Timur's physical appearance makes people want to feed him. And they do feed him. A week after the war began, civilians started coming to the Kyiv volunteer offices bringing food. A lot of food—for the people in the bomb shelters, for the Territorial Defense militia, for the soldiers, for the policemen, and for that poor Russian journalist who sleeps on cardboard boxes in the corner. Timur says that it's a typical Ukrainian reaction to stress: In any unfamiliar situation, they feed everybody who happens to be around. People can't reach their unfortunate compatriots in the basements of occupied Chernihiv, Bucha, and Mariupol, so they feed Timur Olevsky just because he's here.

Three weeks later, Timur leaves Ukraine and goes back to Prague where he finds his editorial office is a wreck. It wasn't an act of physical destruction but an emotional defeat. The people got burned out. Everyone is suffering from PTSD, which affects the quality of their work—it is poor, they get into fights over trifles, and often they can't finish a sentence. Timur tries to bring his colleagues together, thinking it was easier in the war zone. He believes this was his reason for going to war—so as not to go mad. In Prague, Timur begins to understand how much more difficult it is emotionally to watch the catastrophe from the outside than to be physically a part of it.

And then the depression gets him too. As many refugees do, he dreams of going back to his homeland, to Russia, as soon as possible. The moment the political regime changes and the air space reopens, he'll fly back on the first plane. But Timur understands it's not going to happen in the near future. Considering how much he's said and written lately, there's a twenty-year prison sentence waiting for him in Russia.

Eighty Thousand Stories

Unlike Timur Olevsky, Ilya Barabanov, a Russian Service reporter for the BBC, didn't believe there would be war—up to the very last day. Right before the war, he goes to Kharkiv and meets his old acquaintance—the Ukrainian soldier whom he and Timur Olevsky interviewed in Donetsk as a prisoner of the separatists. At that time, this soldier directly accused Russia of provoking and supporting the Donbas conflict with its military forces. Ilya knows this soldier was one of the last prisoners of war exchanged, and that makes him feel guilty: Wasn't this guy kept in the POW camp for an extra year because he gave an honest interview to Baranov and Olevsky? Now this ex-POW smiles and says, "Maybe they kept me one year longer because of you, or maybe they didn't execute me because you made my story known, you said my name, and so they didn't dare put me in front of a firing squad." That's how they talked the day before the war, refusing to believe it could all happen again.

Then Ilya goes to Vovchansk, a small town right on the Russian border, and talks to a local brewer. There are brewers in Vovchansk, but the Nazis, who dominate the region, according to Russian propaganda, are nowhere to be seen. Do you now see why free journalism is a criminal offense in Russia? Because the soldiers of the aggressor's army might learn that their missiles aren't killing Nazis—they're killing brewers. Or *do* the soldiers know it?

From Vovchansk, Ilya returns to Kyiv. He writes his story about the brewer for the BBC and goes to sleep.

In the morning, the doorman tries to wake him up. The doorman thinks Ilya is a British journalist—he's seen how Ilya talks to his colleagues in English, so now he addresses him as Sir: "Sir, we have a war here! Wake up, your colleagues are worried about you. You need to go to a bomb shelter."

Going down into the basement, Ilya sees a Spanish family in the lobby—a mom, a dad, and two children—they must be tourists. The frightened parents are trying to call the Spanish Embassy, but the children are running around the lobby, carefree, playing tag.

Ilya spends the next few days in the bomb shelter or on the balcony of a multi-storey apartment building. He tracks the incoming missiles and reports to his editor where each of the missiles lands. It's a rather strange activity, but it's the essence of a reporter's job: If the world comes to an end, reporters will find the best possible observation point possible and report to their editor: "The first angel sounded his trumpet, and there came hail and fire mixed with blood, and it was hurled down upon the earth. A third of the earth was burned up, a third of the trees were burned up, and all the green grass was burned up."[7]

On the fifth day of the war, the BBC security service informs Ilya that he can't stay in Kyiv any longer. If the Russian troops occupy the city, Ilya won't be treated as a journalist doing his job. The occupiers will see him as a collaborator, and he'll be arrested, taken to Russia, and put in prison for twenty years. Becoming a refugee is a piece of cake for a citizen of the aggressor country, too—all you need to do is be an honest war correspondent.

Together with several British colleagues, Ilya goes west. Their minibus is stopped at every checkpoint, but as soon as the border patrol officers see British passports, they let them go without a search. The Ukrainian soldiers are usually too busy to check all the papers and so don't see Ilya's Russian passport. But it does happen a couple of times—the soldiers pull Ilya out of the minibus and, treating him like a newly captured Russian spy, escort him to their office or directly in front of a firing squad. At this point, Ilya explains that he's a BBC reporter, his colleagues confirm that Ilya is one of them, and after that they're allowed to continue on to Moldova.

Ilya spends quite some time in Kishinev. He needs a Hungarian transit visa to get to Belgrade, and from Belgrade he'll go to Riga, where the full BBC Russian Service is relocating. In addition, Ilya needs to get his wife out of Moscow through Tbilisi.

Theoretically, Ukrainian martial law doesn't allow male citizens to leave the country; the only exception is for fathers of many children and for those with disabilities. Ilya says that at night, all the Kishinev bars are full of these "disabled fathers of large families," looking hale and hearty. Someone must have

---

[7] This is a quotation from *Revelations* 8: 6-7.

allowed them to leave the country. They must have given bribes at the border checkpoints. The Ukrainian border patrol must have taken the bribes, despite the war. That's why no one likes reporters. The Russian authorities don't like them because they find brewers in Vovchansk, and the Ukrainian authorities don't because they find deserters in Kishinev. All the same, the Russian powers that be hate Ilya more than any others.

Ilya specializes in investigating cases involving the Russian Army. He prefers not to get involved in Ukrainian cases. There are enough Ukrainian journalists to discuss their war. Most of the stories Ilya publishes are about Russian soldiers who have perished in various unrighteous wars throughout the world. He won't return to Russia. It doesn't matter to him where he conducts his investigations—it could be in Antarctica, as long as there's a good Internet connection. He's writing a book about the Wagner Private Military Company, whose soldiers are now fighting in Ukraine. He phones the soldiers' wives. At first, the women refuse to talk to Ilya, as they would refuse to talk to an enemy, but when they're informed their husbands are dead, they change their minds. And the stories pile up . . .

Ilya feels sorry for them. For every fallen Russian soldier, he tries to find out the circumstances that led to the soldier's death. According to the most approximate calculations, twenty thousand Russian soldiers have been killed in Ukraine. This means that sixty thousand have been injured. All of them were at some point in their lives children, who loved their mothers, who wanted to have a pet kitten, who sang songs about the sun in kindergarten, dreamt about something, but somehow they learned to be cruel, and this led to their death or mutilation. There are eighty thousand dead and injured, and someone has to tell eighty thousand stories about them. Ilya has to tell those stories.

For his attempts to see those Russian soldiers as human beings, not just cannon fodder, the Russian authorities opened a criminal case with a potential sentence of twenty years in prison.

The President's Interview

There's a much more serious offense in Russia, which also carries a sentence of up to twenty years in prison. It involves not just presenting a Ukrainian civilian, a brewer or a metal worker, as a human being, but attempting to present the Supreme Commander-in-Chief of the Armed Forces of Ukraine, President Zelenskyy, as a human being. Mikhail Zygar, the author of *The Empire Must Die*, is undertaking precisely that.

Mikhail isn't taking part in this war. He used to be a war reporter for the newspaper *Kommersant* in the times of the legendary editor Andrey Vasilyev, but then his career picked up. He was the editor-in-chief of the TV channel Dozhd. Then he created his own studio. He wrote several books on history. And then the war began. And Mikhail left Russia three days later.

First, because he has a daughter. It's obvious that by starting this war, Russia has robbed its citizens of their future, but Mikhail believes his little girl must have a future. His daughter benefits from the situation: Her long-divorced parents move into one apartment in Berlin to live with her—her mom and dad together, something she only dreamed about.

Second, because—as Mikhail formulates it—it's impossible to breathe in a country where fascism has won.

Third, because it's impossible for a journalist to remain silent in a country that has let fascism win. But to speak up is deadly dangerous. By speaking up during the first three days of the war, Misha has already secured a decent prison sentence. On social media platforms, he posted the anti-war petition signed by three hundred thousand people including celebrities like the actress Chulpan Khamatova and the writer Boris Akunin.

On the day of their departure, on the very day that Mikhail, with his ex-wife and daughter, got into a taxi in Moscow to go to the airport, German Chancellor Olaf Scholz closed German airspace to Russian planes. And all other European countries did the same. What could he do? Mikhail thinks that if they decided to leave, then they should leave, so on their way to the airport, he buys the first available tickets for his family—to Dubai, and from there to Berlin.

Mikhail says that on the third day of the war, Moscow's Sheremetyevo airport, named for the poet Alexander Pushkin, looks like an airport after an apocalypse. Not apocalyptic, like the Kabul airport looked after the Taliban took control of the city and all normal Afghanis tried to flee. But post-apocalyptic—when everything is over, and the dead return home, without emotion, from the airport where they had tried to get on flights to Paris, Berlin, or London.

Mikhail settles down in Berlin better than many Russian journalists. He calls himself a lucky loser—it's always like that with him, any personal or professional catastrophe turns out well, becoming an exciting adventure and opening up new opportunities. He writes a weekly column for *Der Spiegel*, finishes two books on history at the same time—one about the formation of Ukraine and the other about the collapse of the Soviet Union—and sets up an interview with the president of Ukraine, Volodymyr Zelenskyy, the only interview granted a Russian journalist since the beginning of the war.

The idea for this interview came from the Russian producer and visionary Ilya Khrzhanovsky. In Ukraine, Khrzhanovsky organized Babiy Yar, an enormous project that includes a museum, theater, and cultural center devoted to one of the most tragic pages of Ukrainian history—the mass extermination of Jews during World War II. Khrzhanovsky negotiates with the administration of President Zelenskyy. The idea is to show that Russians and Ukrainians can communicate. From this interview, it should become obvious to the Ukrainian audience that not all Russian journalists are shameless, propagandistic liars. And for the Russian audience, it should become obvious that the Ukrainian president is neither a Nazi nor a drug addict, as

Russian propaganda presents him, but a rather charming person. He grieves, gets angry, seems puzzled, and almost cries on several occasions, and several times he utters something that no one could ever imagine coming from the lips of the Russian president, that he feels sorry for people. A politician who feels sorry for people.

Four Russian journalists conduct this interview before the Ukrainian army liberates the small town of Bucha, and the atrocious war crimes committed by the Russian troops are discovered—execution, torture, rape. And the impression created by the interview, that Russians and Ukrainians can communicate, is wiped out by the reports from Bucha. And the Russian journalists who conducted that interview, except for Ivan Kolpakov, the editor-in-chief of the Meduza media platform based in Riga, lose their jobs and become pariahs. Here are their names: Tikhon Dzyanko, editor-in-chief of the now shuttered TV channel Dozhd and a good friend of mine; Vladimir Solovyov, a former special correspondent for the newspaper *Kommersant* and also a friend of mine; and Mikhail Zygar, my friend and coauthor.

The President's Speech

In a café on the beach in Jūrmala, Latvia, I'm sitting with Andrey Vasilyev, the above-mentioned editor-in-chief of the newspaper *Kommersant*. Of course, you can't call Andrey a refugee or an exile. He's an émigré, and a very wealthy émigré at that. He's telling me a story about an alternative path—how everything could have gone in a different direction, and how the lives of my refugee characters could have been very different.

At the beginning of the 2000s, when Russia was still a relatively free country, Andrey was probably the highest paid editor-in-chief of what was clearly the most influential newspaper in the country. I worked for him as a special reporter, and it was the happiest time of my professional life. Then freedom in Russia came to an end, and Andrey was laid off, but with a huge "golden parachute"—an unbelievably generous compensation package. He shrugged his shoulders, bought a house on the seaside, and began to lead the life of a retiree. Then, together with the artist Mikhail Yefremov and poets Dmitry Bykov and Andrey Orlov, he created a project known to all democratic protesters in Moscow: *The Citizen Poet.* The project is long closed, Yefremov is in prison (from where he proclaims his support for the war), while Bykov and Orlov are in exile. Andrey again left for Jūrmala to do nothing, but . . . his heart remained in Russia.

"Ha-ha-ha! What are you talking about, Panyushkin?" Andrey gulps his mojito, his fifth, I think. "I don't have a heart!"

He's a cynic and a drunk, but everyone who's ever worked with him knows that Vasilyev is a genius.

Perhaps with that in mind, not long before the war began Ilya Khrzhanovsky came to Vasilyev with a crazy idea: to write a speech for President Zelenskyy that could stop the war. And Vasilyev agreed.

"Can you imagine, Panyushkin," after downing his sixth mojito, "I took it upon myself to stop the war, for real."

"You failed," I answer.

"Oh well!" Vasilyev throws up his hands, perhaps in dismay or perhaps to summon the waiter.

He spent weeks thinking about this speech, then wrote it in three hours, finishing it on February 24, at 4:00 A.M.

"But by that time," Vasilyev says, "there were two double bourbons inside of me. I thought I'd sleep it off and edit the speech in the morning, with a clear head. So, I went to sleep. An hour later, the war began."

The speech that Andrey Vasilyev wrote for Volodymyr Zelenskyy in a desperate attempt to stop the war, was never delivered. I've read that speech. In it, President Zelenskyy suggests having a referendum about giving Donbas to Russia—to give them Donbas, "and let Putin choke on it." Then he announces his resignation after the referendum. And finally, he says that he's not sorry to leave the presidency behind, but he feels sorry for the people who will die fighting for the independence of Ukraine. He feels sorry for the Ukrainian people, but he's sorry for the Russians too.

Even if it had been delivered, I don't think this speech would have stopped the war. Putin wants more than the Donbas; he wants the entire "Russian world."

We're sitting in a café on the beach, and along the shore a famous Russian actor passes by. He's practicing Nordic walking, in an attempt to ward off aging, I presume.

"Are you staying here for long?" Vasilyev asks, calling the actor by name.

The artist turns around:

"It's looking like I'll be here until the end of my life."

The Final Chapter
We're Leaving

> "Since the start of the special military operation, 264 planes, 145 helicopters, 1711 unmanned aircraft, 363 anti-aircraft missile systems, 4278 tanks and other combat armored vehicles, 794 rocket salvo-fire systems, 3284 field artillery weapons and mortars, as well as 4785 special military vehicles have been destroyed." Summary of the Ministry of Defense of the Russian Federation on the progress of the special military operation on the territory of Ukraine, August 9, 2022.

In G-minor

"Are you saying goodbye?" my mother-in-law asks.

I'm sitting in the living room of our house in the suburbs of Moscow and quietly playing the piano. The music is by John Williams from the movie *Schindler's List*. The piano is a Diederichs. In the nineteenth century, the Russian instruments made by the brothers Diederichs were the finest in the word. But the company didn't survive the Revolution, and the piano factories were closed. Any Diederichs piano is therefore of pre-revolutionary origin and so a witness to a time before Russia began destroying itself. I restored this instrument, as if pulling a thread through the previous century, which was so ruinous for Russia, to repair the fabric of time. I restored this instrument, and now I'm playing it for the last time.

"Are you saying goodbye?" says my mother-in-law.

"Yes, I'm saying goodbye."

This last chapter is about me. And it's about feelings. For three months now, I've been writing about people leaving their homeland, and now the time has come for me to do the same.

To be honest, this farewell has been postponed for quite

some time. The war began on February 24, but we're leaving in May. During the first week of the war, I, as well as many of my friends, could find no peace of mind. I couldn't figure out what I should do in a world in which my country attacked the neighboring country where my first wife was from, and my second wife, as well. We're constantly asking one another why this particular war is so intolerable. There have been other wars—aggressive and barbaric in the same way and no less cruel. Russia has been killing people in Afghanistan, and in Chechnya, and in Syria. How were we able to lead normal lives with that in the background? And why are we incapable of leading normal lives now?

I've formulated an answer for myself. I was able to write about those previous wars conducted by Russia because I was a newspaper reporter. I could go to the frontline and send my reports back to the newspaper. I could talk about how people were dying, how mothers were searching for their lost children, about the smell of a blown-up house, how the barely detectable sweetish odor of decaying bodies mixes with the smell of smoke and dust. About how people were changing, how violence is becoming the new ethical norm because "everybody does it." I could write about all of this, and it gave me the strength to survive.

But the Ukrainian war of 2022 differs from all other wars in that the first thing the Russian government did was to prohibit us from even using the word "war." When we left in May, the repressions hadn't reached the level of the deputy Alexey Goryunov. In July, he'll get seven years in prison for calling the war a "war" during a meeting in his municipality and for expressing his disagreement with this war. But even at the end of April, critics of the regime were reported missing to INTERPOL—Alexander Nevzorov, Nika Belozyorskaya . . . And special wartime criminal cases (with prison sentences extended by many years) are being prepared against Vladimir Kara-Murza and

Ilya Yashin.[8] And the possibility of speaking up is shrinking day by day.

In the two months since the war began and before we left, my friend Irina Vorobyova, a journalist for the radio station Ekho Moskvy and for the newspaper *Novaya Gazeta* stopped over twice. She came the first time when Ekho was closed, and the second time when *Novaya* was closed. My friend, a hematologist, came over and told us there were still drugs for his patients but because of the sanctions, his scientific research had ended and wouldn't be possible again any time soon. Another friend, a geneticist, said that genetic research had become impossible. I asked both if they were ready to give interviews about the state of Russian medicine—no, they weren't ready. After such an interview, they'd be forced to quit, but by keeping quiet, they're still able to treat children.

We're surrounded by silence. Two of my school friends fell out because one thinks the war is just, and the other believes it's criminal, so they stopped talking to each other. Before the May holidays, my kids' teacher, whom they adored, wrote in the school chatroom that the children should prepare for a patriotic demonstration. They gave the kids military caps and carnations, so they could march with pride. Every student received a flower. And every one of them had to bring a hundred rubles to school to pay for the carnation. And we didn't object, we didn't protest in the school chatroom against the government trying to brainwash our children, that our children were being lied to and were being taught how to lie. Only my mother-in-law made a sarcastic

---

[8] Vladimir Kara-Murza (b. 1981) is a Russian opposition leader and journalist, and vocal critic of Vladimir Putin. Since February 2022, he has been a member of the Russian Anti-War Committee. He was poisoned in 2015 and 2017, and in October 2022 he was arrested and charged with high treason, which carries a prison term of up to twenty years. Ilya Yashin (b. 1983) is a Russian politician, public figure, and journalist. In December 2022, he was sentenced under Russia's wartime censorship laws to eight and a half years in prison for spreading "fake news" about the Russian Armed Forces.

comment about the announcement, "It seems a bit steep: a hundred rubles for a carnation. In the cemetery, they're half the price."

We're surrounded by silence. Our get-togethers are now like funerals. All our conversations have been reduced to commemorations. At that time, the producer Alexander Syomin, one of the most talented people I know, organized a concert at the House of Actors in Moscow. Sasha wrote a sad minimalist piece of music for a string quintet; the musicians performed and then, in the intermissions between the movements, Sasha read ads from the stage—classified ads about renting, selling, and buying that people had posted on the Internet before the start of the war and after. The audience fell silent, and it felt like a gathering of conspirators.

We took our children to that concert. As I was listening to the music and to Sasha reading the ads, I thought about how I would explain the meaning of those ads to our kids.

"January 2022. For rent, an apartment in Mariupol. First line building, a sea view, two bedrooms, spacious kitchen-living room, built-in appliances. Daily and long-term rents possible."

You know, kids, Mariupol used to be a resort city. People would go there on vacation, to swim in the sea, to eat fresh fish. Now Mariupol is destroyed, there are no longer houses on the seashore. And those two bedrooms and spacious kitchen-living room are probably in ruins.

The musicians played. Sasha kept reading. He didn't explain anything; he just read the ads.

"March 2022. Belgorod. For sale: two used rugs in good condition."

You see, kids, after capturing Ukrainian cities, the Russian soldiers were looting, stealing everything they could get their hands on, even small things—irons, teapots, washers, rugs. And later, when they returned to Russia, they tried to sell these used goods.

Sasha read, and the music played. In the concert program, there was a line in a small font: "** ***"

Do you understand, kids, what that means? Everyone in Moscow understands—it means "NO WAR," kids. We're even prohibited from saying "No war."

The day after the concert, someone sent a report about the performance to the FSB, the post-Soviet version of the KGB: *Alexander Syomin organized an anti-Russian action at the House of Actors—they played music and he read ads. The word "war" wasn't mentioned, but it was implied.* And the program with the little stars was included.

At about the same time, I got the idea for this book, and it became easier to breathe. With each new chapter, with each new interview I conducted for this book I felt, on the one hand, that I could still be useful, while on the other hand, I understood more and more clearly that this book couldn't be published in Russia. It's not even because of the danger of prison time facing the author of a book about refugees. The problem is: I'd never find a publisher.

If I stay in Russia, no one will ever know about the characters in this book—about Alla who sees a castle in her dream, about Denys who drives from Mariupol on flat tires, about Danya whose brother perishes in the war, about Nadezhda Ivanovna who listens to her dog howling . . . Silence will envelop them and me. And the saddest thing of all is that we will gradually get used to that silence. First, we'll get used to being silent about us starting this war. Then we'll get used to the thought that we probably didn't start the war, and if the war was started, it wasn't us who started it. And finally, even if we manage to preserve our memory and avoid Stockholm syndrome, we will surely be unable to protect our children from the false belief instilled in them by the government that we were the ones who were attacked, as they'd like the entire world to believe.

That's why we're leaving.

It goes without saying that the way we're leaving our homeland can't be compared to how the Ukrainian refugees—tortured by hunger, cold, and bombardment—are leaving their homeland. Yes, but it's possible to run away from bombs; humanitarian organizations can feed the hungry, and Rubikus volunteers can place the frozen in the warm houses of host families. But what can you do with the feeling of guilt? With the burning feeling of guilt and shame of being a citizen of the aggressor country? What can you do with the fact that the people I live with call evil good and darkness light?

It's also sad to see how easily the old people, who back in Soviet times were trained to accept the lies, have resurrected that peculiar skill of seeing lies as the truth. Like my father, for example.

Lost Opportunities

My wife's small car is loaded to the roof with our children's toys. We sold my car to pay off debts. My in-laws will live in our house for now, but only until the winter. In winter, my wife's parents refuse to live in the suburbs, and I don't know what will happen then.

The children hug their grandma and grandpa. They're eleven, ten, and five years old—two girls and one boy. My mother-in-law is crying. The children are crying too as they get in the car, but soon they're distracted by a territorial dispute of their own. It's not enough space for all of them in the back seat, and my younger son is trying to find a seat for Hagi-Vagi, his favorite toy—a plush blue monster with a toothy smile from ear to ear.

"Why don't you put your Hagi-Vagi in the trunk?" the girls hiss at their brother.

"No, Hagi-Vagi stays here with me!"

My dog approaches. My big black mutt that looks like a pointer. He seems sad but tries to behave.

"It's not your fault, buddy. I'll come back for you." This is what I say to my dog, but honestly, I don't know whether I'll come back or not.

We get in the car and drive. The lilacs are blooming, and tulips . . . there are many, many tulips. Out of the seventeen million square meters of Russian land, I managed to develop less than a hectare—my house and my garden.

The dog runs after our car. I can see him in the rear-view mirror. He runs as far as the intersection and, as if figuring out—*No, they won't take me with them!*—sits down at the intersection and watches us go. He doesn't bark, he doesn't howl—he just watches. My son turns back and waves at the dog with his Hagi-Vagi: "Bye! We'll come back for you!"

But I don't know whether we can come back.

We're driving through land that is blossoming in spring. The birch groves are shimmering in the sunlight, but the fields are barely plowed. The fields of northern Russia are mostly covered in hogweed shoots. Among all possible human activities, my homeland has recently chosen oil production and waging wars. There are many vehicles with the letter "Z" driving in the opposite direction. Most of them are municipal vehicles—garbage trucks and intercity buses; private citizens are not as eager to write that cursed letter on their cars. The state does it.

It's a long trip. The children get tired. We won't make it to Riga in a single day, so we stop in Pskov to spend the night. We take advantage of this to take the children to see the Pskov Kremlin. Look, children, this is Veche Square. Do you know what "veche" means? Do you know that this used to be a republic? A very long time ago, Russia was able to govern itself not by the Horde autocracy of one cruel man, but by the democratic votes of free people. We lost this opportunity. We lost many opportunities. We even use alphabet letters for wrong purposes—to scare our neighbors.

The Border

The next morning, we approach the Russian-Estonian border, and my son sticks his Hagi-Vagi's nose against the window to watch a line of trucks many kilometers long. This is a noticeable effect of the international economic sanctions against Russia. The drivers talk about eating, drinking, and taking a shower on the Estonian side because, on the Russian side, there are no cafés or showers. There's no place to eat, to wash up, there aren't even any bathrooms—the drivers go to the nearest woods, which is full of snakes. If a snake bites someone in the woods, an ambulance can come from the Estonian side, but not from the Russian side—it's a closed border zone.

The line for cars is not as long—we're eighth or ninth. The characters in my book, the Ukrainian refugees, have to cross the border by foot. They've come by bus and, on the Estonian side, they hope to get on another bus. The car owners contemptuously refer to the refugees as "those people." "Oh, I hope there won't be any of those people today." "That's it, those people are here. Now they'll have to check each of them for at least half an hour, and we'll have to wait." As if the refugees themselves demanded these hour-long inspections. As if it's not Russia who kicked them out of their homes. As if they decided to travel through Europe just for fun.

There's a little yard near the border checkpoint—three evergreen trees, two benches, and an ash tray. As we wait our turn, my children play in the yard, and Hagi-Vagi climbs a tree.

Suddenly, a nice expensive car appears out of nowhere. A sprightly fellow jumps out and greets everyone in the line, even the children. He shakes everyone's hands and says that he's terribly late for his flight—the plane will be taking off literally in a couple of hours from the Tallinn airport. Of course, he's lying, but he does so with great enthusiasm! In an instant, literally, he convinces everyone in the line to let him pass, the customs officer to inspect his car as fast as possible, and the female border patrol agent to stamp his passport without wasting any time. I look at this fella and think—he's just like Vovan. Remember the driver who took people across the frontline in Ukraine? He had to deal with Russian as well as Ukrainian soldiers, and he could get through places no one could imagine. Here he is, my Vovan.

We wait in line for three hours then cross the border in three minutes. The border patrol officers are giving me the cold shoulder. The female officer who was just smiling and chatting with the sprightly fellow, looks at me with contempt:

"The border is closed. You know that Russia's land border is closed, don't you?"

Actually, she's lying too. Our papers are in order, and she has no right to keep us from leaving. But for several minutes she exerts power over us, and she is thoroughly enjoying her little power game:

"Wait! You aren't going anywhere yet!"

With these words, she takes our passports and returns fifteen minutes later with our passports stamped.

"Kids, get in the car, quick! We're leaving."

We cross the Estonian border quickly, in no more than ten minutes. In Estonia, we stop for a smoke on the side of the road. You can still see the Russian influence here—there are cigarette butts all over the roadside and in the ditch and used paper cups with the letter "Z." Everything will be clean from here on.

The older girls are laughing and singing a song they made up, "We left Putin behind," but suddenly my son screams:

"Hagi-Vagi! Where's my Hagi-Vagi?! I left it in the pine tree in the other country! In that courtyard! I left it! Hagi-Vagi!"

And there are tears in his eyes. I begin to realize that I might have to cross the Russian-Estonian border two more times—there and back. We can't leave Hagi-Vagi behind, can we?

The girls try to comfort their brother:

"Don't cry! Daddy'll go and get Hagi-Vagi. Don't worry, we won't lose him."

"Hagi-Vagi!" our little boy is unconsolable.

I'm smoking and thinking about how in a few moments I'll reach the Russian border, leave the car there, and . . . It'll probably be impossible to convince the border patrol officers that I'm going back for just a few minutes to find a toy my son left behind. So, I'll have to go through inspection again, follow all the protocols, and tolerate the fifteen-minute exercise of power by that female border patrol officer. And one more thought pounds in the depth of my conscience and tortures me—the scary thought that they might let me back into Russia but not allow me to leave again. Why would they not allow me to leave? But the thought continues to pound in my brain.

"Hagi-Vagi!" my son is screaming.

"In a second, in a second, I'll go and bring him back"

"Hagi-Vagi!" the tone is different this time: It's a happy voice. "He's here! He got under the seat, dad. He was under the seat! He's here!"

"Hagi-Vagi! Hoorah!" The children are hugging and laughing as if everything that could possibly go wrong is now behind them. And they're singing "Hagi-Vagi is found" to the tune of "Happy Birthday to You." "Hagi-Vagi is found!"

"Okay," my wife says, "it's time to get going."

I put out my cigarette and place the butt in my pocket, to avoid littering. I get in the car and turn on the engine.

"Is everyone buckled up? Okay, let's go."

And now I don't have a homeland either.

THE END
2022
Amelfino
Amatciems
Riga

About the Author

Valery Panyushkin is a journalist and writer, the author of thirteen books, including *12 Who Don't Agree: The Battle for Freedom in Putin's Russia* (Europa, 2011). Born in Leningrad in 1969, he has left Russia and currently lives abroad.

EUROPA EDITIONS UK

READ THE WORLD

Literary fiction, popular fiction, narrative non-fiction,
travel, memoir, world noir

Building bridges between cultures with the finest writing from around the world.

Ahmet Altan, Peter Cameron, Andrea Camilleri, Catherine Chidgey,
Sandrine Collette, Christelle Dabos, Donatella Di Pietrantonio, Négar Djavadi,
Deborah Eisenberg, Elena Ferrante, Lillian Fishman, Anna Gavalda,
Saleem Haddad, James Hannaham, Jean-Claude Izzo, Maki Kashimada,
Nicola Lagioia, Alexandra Lapierre, Grant Morrison, Ondjaki, Valérie Perrin,
Christopher Prendergast, Eric-Emmanuel Schmitt, Domenico Starnone,
Esther Yi, Charles Yu

*Acts of Service, Didn't Nobody Give a Shit What Happened to Carlotta,
Ferocity, Fifteen Wild Decembers, Fresh Water for Flowers, Lambda,
Love in the Days of Rebellion, My Brilliant Friend, Remote Sympathy,
Sleeping Among Sheep Under a Starry Sky, Total Chaos, Transparent City,
What Happens at Night, A Winter's Promise*

Europa Editions was founded by Sandro Ferri and Sandra Ozzola,
the owners of the Rome-based publishing house Edizioni E/O.

Europa Editions UK is an independent trade publisher
based in London.

www.europaeditions.co.uk

Follow us at . . .
Twitter: @EuropaEdUK
Instagram: @EuropaEditionsUK
TikTok: @EuropaEditionsUK